SEVEN
TO BUY THIS BOOK

1. PROPHESY
We sit at the eve of events that are certain to occur literally:
just as literally as the Flood, the birth of Jesus Christ,
and the Regathering of Israel.

2. PROGNOSTICATORS
If you don't know one or two, where have you been?
Ours is a world filled with dishonest teachers.

3. A NEW APPROACH-DEMONSTRATED
This book shows you how to locate the movements that
the Apostle Paul intended the reader to discover.

4. EXAMPLES
Illustrations from secular literature aid in understanding
the genre of letters. Three are included in this book.

5. ONE SOURCE OPINION
In many useful volumes, one wonders who the real author
is. Is it the name on the cover or the hundreds of sources
quoted in the text? Many books are just a compilation of
unendorsed research.

6. GREEK
The Greek text is included for your perusal.
As A.T. Robertson wrote,
"The Greek New Testament is the New Testament".

7. PRINTED REFERENCES
It would seem that if a verse was really worth citing, it might be
worth printing. To facilitate and thereby aid learning,
the references have been printed.

THESSALONIKI: THE GATEWAY TO PROPHETIC EVENTS

A CONCISE COMMENTARY
BASED ON THE LITERARY STRUCTURE OF
1 & 2 THESSALONIANS

BY GREGORY E. MAFFIN

Bookstand Publishing
www.bookstandpublishing.com

THESSALONIKI:
THE GATEWAY TO PROPHETIC EVENTS
Published by Bookstand Publishing
© 2011 Gregory E. Maffin
1. Bible. N.T.- Prophesy 2. N.T.- 1 & 2 Thessalonians
3330_3

ISBN: 978-1-58909-910-4

Cover Image by award winning artist Mark Maffin
All Bible references contained herein are from the KJV
or the author's translation. Other translations referenced as cited.
All Greek quotations are from The New Testament in the Original Greek,
by Brooke Foss Westcott D.D. and Fenton John Anthony Hort D.D.
(London, Macmillan and Co.), 1900. Author's copy.
Printed in the United States of America

For information contact
Bookstand Publishing
A Division of FastPress Publishing Inc.
305 Vineyard Town Center, Suite 302
Morgan Hill, CA 95037 USA
Phone: 866-793-9365 or 408-852-1832
Fax: 408-413-5443
Email: support@bookstandpublishing.com

Dedicated to my dad,
My Hero

TABLE OF CONTENTS

Phase 3

Executing the Methods and
Observations Learned in the First Two
Phases on the Thessalonian letters
- Locate elements
- Locate sections
- Dig into the arguments and
  applications of the text

CHAPTER ONE

THE ROOTS OF THE LETTER

Paul wrote his letters on papyrus (παπυρος, stalk): a paper made from the papyrus stalk. It was a reed that grew in the delta of the Nile. In water about three feet deep, this reed at its root was as thick as a man's arm and reached in length, around fifteen feet long (Theophrastus). It was in general use six hundred years before Christ. Papyrus roots were used for firewood, and the manufacture of furniture, piths, sails, mats, clothing, coverings and rope. The stalks also made boats (such as Moses floated in Ex 2:3, **And when she could not longer hide him, she took for him an ark of bulrushes, and daubed it with slime and with pitch, and put the child therein; and she laid it in the flags by the river's brink**). It is also mentioned in Isaiah 18:2, **papyrus boats.**

Papyrus paper is mentioned in the NT (2 Jn 12, **with paper and ink** [χάρτου καὶ μέλανος]). The manufacturing process of papyrus paper is considerable. The stalk part of the reed would be cut into thin, broad strips, moistened with paste and doubled at right angles. Upon being soaked with water, it would be beaten or pressed into a substance resembling paper. These sheets "thus formed were again pressed, trimmed into uniform sizes, dried carefully in the sun, and finally polished down with a shell or piece of ivory". Metzger notes "In writing on papyrus the scribe was accustomed to utilize the horizontal fibers on the recto side of the sheet as guide lines for his script". Unlike books of today, the sheets would be pasted together to form a roll. The standard size would be

Papyrus Bodmer II (p66) 200 C.E.

twenty sheets stretching thirty-nine feet. Some have estimated the Gospel of Luke at thirty one feet long. The inner end of the roll was fastened to a roller tipped with a simple button or ivory horn while the outer end was sometimes glued to a similar strip. The process of making paper from papyrus reeds has not passed. The process is demonstrated on line and papyrus paper can be purchased - at an elevated cost.

The written form of a letter or document would consist of parallel columns at right angles. The lines generally averaged thirty-eight letters with no spacing between words. Shorter letters would be folded and the name of the addressee would be printed on the outside– serving as its own envelope.

The inscribing instrument would be a "hollow reed pen" (3 Jn 13, **with ink and pen** [καλάμου]). It was cut to a point and split like a quill even in the earliest times. Some pens of this shape have been found made of silver and bronze.

Black ink was made of vegetable soot and would be mixed with a "gummy medium", molded and dried like India ink. When writing, one would rub up the solution with water to begin. Finer liquid ink was also used, being made of nutgalls, sulphate of iron and gum.

Red ink was used for "headings, first lines, titles, and marginal notes...." Royal purple ink appears on prized manuscripts late in the third century. Metzger cites a scribal notation, "He who does not know how to write supposes it to be no labor; but though only three fingers write, the whole body labors".

Four hundred years after Christ, papyrus paper was replaced by parchment (coarser varieties of animal skin) and vellum (finer grades of parchment)- more durable, erasable and cheaper. The introduction of paper in its contemporary form appears to have reached the West in the eighth century.

The actual papyrus manuscripts touched by the authors, called the autographs, has not survived time. Although, the transmission of the text has most certainly survived time and circumstances.

There are about twenty thousand manuscripts from the second century to the fifteenth century. These include Siniaticus, Vaticanus, uncials, lectionaries, etc. Utilizing these manuscripts were the Greek editions. These include Stephanus, Westcott-Hort, Nestle and Aland and others. Editions were composed by comparing the readings of available manuscripts and printing the chosen reading - a process called textual criticism. These all reflect the astounding consistency found throughout the scribal history.

Nothing truly compares well with the original languages. Attempting to convert all the nuances of truth from the Greek language over to the English language always results in some loss. It should always be remembered that "An interpretation from a translation, is an interpretation from an interpretation". Most people hold in their hands only a translation of one of the Greek editions. Many of these translations do not attempt to revisit the Greek text for accuracy. The Creator chose a profound language to convey his truth. As A.T. Robertson stated, "The Greek New Testament is the New Testament".

An example from Codex Siniaticus.
An uncial ms written on parchment.

Adapted from George Sitterly,
Praxis in Manuscripts of the Greek Testament, 1898.

CHAPTER TWO

OUTLINING LETTERS: A BRIDGE TO NOWHERE

A few years ago I took up the task of sifting through my books, files and syllabi. Every so often I jettison items that are just ballast along for the ride. I was somewhat surprised at the group of syllabi I discarded. In seminary, the classes most men looked forward to were the book studies. These classes focused on digging into the actual biblical text and mining truth through the original languages. One would suppose these syllabi to be rather valuable. They were an additional charge. Ironically though, all but one of these syllabi I discarded. I knew the reason. They were just large outlines with exegetical points filled in throughout. They did not contain a clear reflection of what the biblical author intended.

The traditional method of outlining is no longer to be preferred as the best presentation of the movements within a Pauline letter. Although books, commentaries and Sunday School lessons seem to require an outline, letters, as in every generation, follow the form of that culture. Recently, I sat down with a Bible college student and explained the structure of a Pauline letter using one of the Greco-Roman letters to follow. Even though he had read and studied the Bible from his youth, his eyes lit up as he finally found a 'handle' with which to grasp the information in Paul's letters.

Traditional outlining has many weaknesses. Typically, it groups topical matter together and often ignores the indicated grammatical and rhetorical movements indicated by the author. It should come as no surprise that it is common for outlines to break Greek sentences into pieces: one part in one division and another part in another division. Such divisions are indefensible as the sentence is the basic unit of communication. A classic example is Phil 4:1 which begins with **so that**, indicating that verse one belongs with the content in chapter three and not chapter four. A crude example may help expose the issue at hand. Years ago I spotted a bumper sticker that read as follows:

Auntie Em,
Hate you,
Hate Kansas,
p.s., Taking the dog

This contrived "letter" had the intended effect; I laughed heartily. Yet, if one were to outline this letter as follows, a disappointing metamorphosis occurs.

I Dorothy Hates Auntie Em
II Dorothy Hates Kansas
III Dorothy Hates Cats (?!?)

Note how outlining simply labels information and eliminates its original form.

Humor, the intention of the bumper sticker, is fully taken away. The same is also true of outlining a Pauline letter; intent and form are stripped away.

Many outlines dutifully follow the chapter divisions and divide the text at the incorrect place. These arbitrary divisions obscure the author's discourse. A good example is Paul's long treatise in Romans on the revealed righteousness of God. It is one unit (1:18-11:36), improperly divided many, many times. Chapter and verse divisions were added about a thousand years after the originals were penned. They carry no weight and should not be used as a guide to dividing the text.

No epistle was written from an outline. Among the thousands of ancient epistles, biblical and non-biblical, no evidence has been advanced that letters were based on or utilized outlines. Even today, when writing a letter, thoughts of constructing an outline are completely absent. It is not a part of the process or the product. It logically follows that what has not been buried in the fabric of the letter cannot be unearthed. Searching for the outline of a Pauline letter is a red herring affair. It should be stated at this point that **sermon outlines have nothing to do with this discussion**. Sermon outlines are topical– they are all based on the singular proposition of the speaker.

Traditional outlining is often a reflection of the writer of the outline rather than the organization of the written work. Divisions in outlines often vary indiscriminately. Labels of those divisions are required to be unique to each writer. Added to this is the unnecessary burden of alliteration, symmetry, and condense and expand steps. Consequently, outlines are all different, none normative. **The result is itself a unique literary work**.

> Letters are multi purpose communiqués that follow the patterns and conventions normal within their culture and are tailored to the purpose for which they are penned. While the content of Paul' letters is unique,
> the style is somewhat common.

Paul's thirteen letters, comprising eighty-seven chapters of the New Testament, are written in similar form to the letters of the Greco-Roman world. Recognizing the form of his writing greatly aids in understanding the content he intends to convey. It may come as a surprise to some that the letters of the New Testament have divisions that the writer, Paul, John and others incorporated into the text. In the three letters exegeted in this book, it will be demonstrated that form and content are inseparable.

Paul's letters are an expanded form of the Greco-Roman letters of his day. This book gives three examples of non Pauline letters (Hermocrates to Chaeras, Apolinarius to Taesis, Diodora to Valerius Maximus). These are given to help the reader see the ancient form and then use it to aid in finding the divisions that Paul intended his readers to discern. Some of the comparisons are rather striking when observed for the first time.

Paul wrote letters for the same reason that people write letters today– a need to write arises. This is why Pauline epistles are termed "occasional". The reasons vary greatly from argumentative letters (Ga) to a letter of report (Phil).

The ancient form of a personal letter divides into three major categories: the **opening, body** and **closing.** The opening usually consists of a prescript and exordium. Sometimes, such as in the pastoral epistles, these are meshed together. In more formal letters, such as to a church, the prescript and exordium are separate and easily distinguishable. The **prescript** contains elements such as the author, co-sponsors, recipients and grace and peace wishes.

The **exordium,** defined as the section preceding the main section, usually starts with thanksgiving or "blessed" and may include a prayer. The relationship between the writer and the recipient often comes to the forefront in this section. As can be seen in the letter of Hermocrates, the exordium can be very positive while the occasion for writing (topic) is very negative. Since the exordium often resembles a long run-on sentence containing many topics, it is an easy place to get lost (Eph 1:3-14). *The exordium is not the occasion for the letter.* Letters are multi purpose– they contain manifold ideas and purposes. The prevalent thesis mind-set that every idea is linked from the first word to the last word must be consciously avoided when approaching the exordium.

The **body** of Paul's letters generally divides into two sections: the **topic** and the **parenesis.** The topic provides the reason for the existence of the letter. Sometimes a disclosure formula indicates explicitly what the writer's purpose was (1 Cor 1:10ff). It should be understood that the term topic does not necessarily denote a theological thesis. Paul's topic could be to report his activities and welfare or wage a doctrinal fight as in Galatians. The topic section can also contain several topics, such as will be seen in I Thessalonians.

Expect the Pauline letters to contain a careful structure. Schreiner

The second part of the body, the **parenesis,** refers to moral injunctions, usually in the form of commands. These can be directly related to the topic, address a local issue, or be general in nature such as house codes. Many sermons utilize these directives since they easily transition to the application level.

Like modern letters, the **closing** of a letter can contain a variety of information. The author is trying to tie up all the loose ends and say the things that are pertinent, yet not worthy to be in the topic section. Salutations, travel plans, closings arguments, and a number of other smaller sections often comprise the closing.

To work with a letter, you may try the approach that I use. I copy and paste the entire Greek text into a desk top publishing program. Verse and chapter divisions are removed as they are no help whatsoever. The text is then broken down into sentences: main clauses (**bold**), subordinate clauses and coordinate clauses aligned correctly. It should be mentioned that Paul did not pen sentences cohering to our English grammar. Sentences or elements (e.g., a grace wish) are grouped into sections which are then bracketed (e.g., parenesis). All divisions must be justified, that is, something in the text must indicate the division. I Corinthians 1 is a good place to practice identifying the opening and the beginning of the body of a letter. To work with the closing of a letter one can dissect Colossians 4:7-18.

CHAPTER THREE

HERMOCRATES AND YOU

I find it much more helpful to use examples from secular literature than to simply ask a group of students to turn in the Bible, to say, Philippians. The reason for this is academic, most believers have read Philippians and been taught it many, many times - using outlines of course. Therefore, they possess a plethora of conclusions and assumptions that hinder them from seeing the epistolary form. A study of these three secular examples will help students of the Bible identify the form found in Paul's thirteen letters.

EXAMPLE 1: HERMOCRATES TO CHAERAS

Hermocrates to Chaeras his son, greeting.	**OPENING** PRESCRIPT
Before all things I pray that you are in health.... I beg you... to write concerning your health and whatever you wish.	EXORDIUM
Some time ago I wrote you concerning the.... and you neither answered nor came and now if you do not come, I run the risk of losing the plot (of land) which I possess. Our partner did not help with the work, for, in truth, not only was the well not cleaned out, but in addition the water channel was filled with sand, and the whole land lies uncultivated. Not one of the tenants was willing to work it– only I continue to pay the public taxes without receiving anything in return– for hardly a single plot does the water irrigate.	**BODY** TOPIC
Therefore, because of necessity, come; otherwise the plants are in danger of perishing.	PARENESIS
Your sister Helene greets you, and your mother reproaches you because you did not answer her.	**CLOSING** GREETINGS
Above all, security is demanded by the taxgatherers because you did not send the taxgatherers to you (?) but also now sent to her.	PERORATIO (CLOSING ARGUMENT)
I pray that you are well. Pauni 9. [I. A.D.]	HEALTH WISH

The second example concerns a soldier reporting his situation and orders to his mother. It contains several noteworthy items such as the disclosure formula which begins the topic section- *I wish you to know.* Note the directives in the parenesis, *look after yourself.... Please write.*

EXAMPLE 2: APOLLINARIUS TO TAESIS

Apollinarius to Taesis, his mother and lady, many greetings!

OPENING
PRESCRIPT

Before all I pray for your health. I myself am well, and make supplication for you before the gods of this place.

EXORDIUM

I wish you to know, mother, that I arrived in Rome in good health on the 20th of the month Pachon, and was posted to Misenum, though I have not yet learned the name of my company (kenturian); for I had not gone to Misenum at the time of writing this letter.

BODY
TOPIC

I beg you then, mother, look after yourself and do not worry about me; for I have come to a fine place. Please write me a letter about your welfare and that of my brothers and of all your folk. And whenever I find a messenger I will write to you; never will I be slow to write.

PARENESIS

Many salutations to my brothers and Apollinarius and his children, and Karalas and his children. I salute Ptolemaeus and Ptolemais and her children and Heraclous and her children. I salute all who love you, each by name.

CLOSING
GREETINGS

I pray for your health.

HEALTH WISH

Select Papyri I (1932) #111 (II. A.D.)

W ith the third example is added some Greek for comparison. The letter to the Philippians shows just how current the form of Paul's letter was.

EXAMPLE 3: DIODORA TO VALERIUS MAXIMUS

Diodora to Valerius Maximus, Greetings (χαιϱειν) *and continuous good health* (δια παντος υγιαι-νειν).

Paul's letters open with the author, Paul, and move quickly to the recipients. 3 Jn 2, I **wish above all things that thou mayest prosper and be in health** (ὑγιαίνειν).

I want you to know (γινωσκιν σε θελω) *that we reached the metropolis after nine days, / and straightway I went up to (see) your sister. And straightway, I am writing to you that I am all right* (απϱοσκοπος), *and were kept safe with the gods' will* (εσωθημεν των θηων θελοντων).

The topic section in Philippians also opens with a disclosure formula using several similar terms (1:12, Γινώσκειν δὲ ὑμᾶς βού-λομαι). Like the secular example, it is also a letter reporting the current situation– **Now, I want you to know, brethren, that the things which happened unto me have fallen out rather unto the furtherance of the gospel.**

Greet (ασπαζου) *Amas, / Paulina, Publius, Diodoros, Granias, and Tsche.*
And write to me...
If I settle the business in hand and I'm / all right, I will quickly sail down (ταχυ καταπλευσω).
1 Phaophi (Φαωφι α) *(= 28/29 September).*

Farewell (εϱωσο).
Give this to Maximus (αποδες Μαξιμω) *from Diodoroa (verso)*

Many of Paul's letter offer greetings or salutations (4:21-22). Philippians also contains travel information, as does Titus 3:12, **When I send Artemas to you, or Tychicus, be diligent to come to me at Nicopolis, for I have determined to spend the winter there.** Note how the letter adds a smaller issue in, *If I settle the business....* Secular letters contained a date– something many Bible scholars wished biblical letters contained. Often letters were written on papyrus paper and then folded into an envelope form and addressed: give this to....

G. H. R. Horsley. *New Documents Illustrating Early Christianity.* Macquarie University, 1982 (Vol 1, p 54).

The content of Paul's letters is unique.
The form, however,
is somewhat common.

If we must use the form of an outline, let us incorporate the elements of the text and allow the content to speak for itself. Below is an outline that attempts just that. The letter Pi (π) is used as a general marker for elements and movements within sections.

EXAMPLE 4: PAUL'S LETTER TO THE PHILIPPIANS

I OPENING (1:1-11)

Prescript (1:1-2)
(π) Author, Co-Sponsor (Timothy), Credentials, and Recipients (1:1)
(π) Grace and Peace Wish (1:2)
(π) Exordium: Thanksgiving and prayer for them and their cooperative work (1:3-11).

II BODY (1:12-4:1)

Topic(s) (1:12-2:30)
(π) The gospel proceeds regardless of personal circumstances (1:12-14).
(π) The gospel proceeds regardless of personal motives (1:15-26).
(π) We must live worthy of the gospel (1:27-30).
(π) Be unified (2:1-11).
(π) Be active (2:12-18).
(π) Anticipate Timothy's coming (2:19-24).
(π) Receive Epaphroditus (2:25-30).

Parenesis (3:1-4:1)
(π) Beware of the Jews! (3:1-12)
(π) Press toward the mark! (3:13-16)
(π) Mimic me! (3:17-4:1)

III CLOSING (4:2-23)
(π) Personal instructions (4:2-3)
(π) Final injunctions (4:4-7)
(π) Peroratio: final discussion (4:8-9)
(π) Personal situations (4:10-19)

Postscript (4:20-23)
(π) Benediction (4:20)
(π) Salutations (4:21-22)
(π) Grace Wish (4:23)

I prefer to use a visual presentation that is far removed from the associations caused by seeing the outline form. This diagram illustrates the schema, or underlying organizational pattern, found in Titus.

EXAMPLE 5: PAUL'S LETTER TO TITUS

SCHEMA
OF TITUS

OPENING	BODY	CLOSING

PRESCRIPT
AND
EXORDIUM
(1:1-4)

TOPIC:

[ALPHA]
APPOINTMENT
OF ELDERS
(1:5-16)

[BETA]
ESTABLISHMENT
OF THE PEOPLE
(2:1-15)

POST-
SCRIPT
(3:12-15)

PARENESIS
(3:1-11)

† columns and font sizes are proportional to the text

And finally, I have added summary information to this schema. This information serves as an introduction to the letter. It should be noted that this style of presentation is by no means the only useful method of illustration.

EXAMPLE 5: PAUL'S LETTER TO THE COLOSSIANS

...OPENING ...

| PRESCRIPT (1:1-2) | EXORDIUM (1:3-16a) |

EXORDIUM
(1:3-16a)
This section usually starts with thanksgiving (vv 3-8) or blessed be. The second element is often prayer (v 9ff). Only Galatians does not contain an exordium. The exordium reflects the relationship between the writer and recipient and often hints at what the letter will say. The form of the exordium can be problematic since it often translates as a run-on sentence. Many readers lose their way in this section.

...BODY ...

TOPIC
(1:16b–2:23)
The topic section constitutes the section that carries the purpose of the letter; it is the reason why the letter was generated. It should not be assumed that this section carries a thesis. In Colossians, there are several suggested starting points for the topic. With no disclosure formula to lean upon, the starting point is debatable. Why here (16b)? Although in the midst of a verse, the sentence is an independent clause. Also, when Paul addressed the Epicurean and Stoic philosophers at the Areopagus, his first salvo is, God who made the world and everything in it…. It seems that after the digression on the Father beginning in v 12 and his dear son in v 14, Paul begins his support for the truth starting with the creative work of Jesus and the creative purpose: Jesus.

PARENESIS
(3:1-4:6)
The word parenesis means to exhort, to advise. Usually this exhortation is in the form of commands. The relationship between the topic and the parenesis should be closely examined. The commands can be borne out of the topic (Phm) or be very general, even detached. In Colossians, this section only lightly reflects upon the topic.

| HAUSTAFELN House codes (3:18-4:1) |

HAUSTAFELN
House codes (3:18-4:1)

...CLOSING ...

POSTSCRIPT
(4:7-18)
Like letters today, the post script contains many elements. These are not of enough concern to be the topic of the letter, but are still necessary for the reader. These include: Paul's Affairs, Couriers, Greetings, Commendation of Co-Laborers, Epistolary Instructions, Note of Validity, Closing Injunction, and a Grace Wish.

CHAPTER FOUR

A WORKING METHOD: PHILEMON

Theologically speaking, Philemon is not the heavyweight that Paul's other epistles are. However, it is a magnificently tailored letter (an "exquisite relic") offering the reader a window into Pauline form in just three hundred forty-five words. Its simplicity and brevity make it the very best place to begin to harvest Pauline literature *according to the movements the author intended*. Utilizing a smaller, simple text as a model will furnish skills that can be used to probe Paul's other, more complex letters.

SCHEMA OF PHILEMON

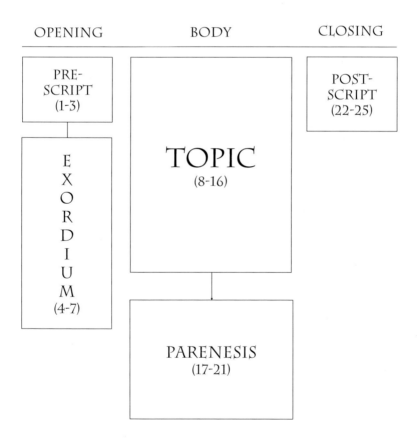

OPENING   BODY   CLOSING

PRE-SCRIPT (1-3)

EXORDIUM (4-7)

TOPIC (8-16)

PARENESIS (17-21)

POST-SCRIPT (22-25)

PHILEMON SKETCHED
PRESCRIPT 1-3
[1-2][π]

Paul, a prisoner of Christ Jesus and Timothy the brother, to the beloved Philemon and our co-worker, and to Apphia our sister, and to Archippus our fellow soldier, and to the church in your house.

[3][π]

Grace to you and peace from God our Father and the Lord Jesus Christ.

Main clauses: BOLD, Subordinate/Coordinate elements: ITALICS

REFERENCES
[1][π]

(Phil 1:21) For to me to live is Christ, and to die is gain.

(Eph 1:21ff) Far above all principality, and power, and might, and dominion, and every name that is named, not only in this world, but also in that which is to come: [22] And hath put all things under his feet, and gave him to be the head over all things to the church, [23] Which is his body, the fullness of him that filleth all in all.

(Jn 19:11) Jesus answered, Thou couldest have no power at all against me, except it were given you from above....

(Eph 3:15) Of whom the whole family in heaven and earth is named

[2]

(2 Tim 2:3-4) Thou therefore endure hardness, as a good soldier of Jesus Christ. [4] No man that warreth entangleth himself with the affairs of this life; that he may please him who hath chosen him to be a soldier.

(Phil 2:25) Yet I supposed it necessary to send to you Epaphroditus, my brother, and companion in labor, and fellow soldier, but your messenger, and he that ministered to my wants.

(Ro 16:3-5) Greet Priscilla and Aquila my helpers in Christ Jesus: [4] Who have for my life laid down their own necks: unto whom not only I give thanks, but also all the churches of the Gentiles. [5] Likewise greet the church that is in their house. Salute my well-beloved Epaenetus, who is the first fruits of Achaia unto Christ.

(Col 4:15) Salute the brethren which are in Laodicea, and Nymphas, and the church which is in his house.

[3][π]

(Eph 2:14ff) For he is our peace, who hath made both one, and hath broken down the middle wall of partition between us; [15] Having abolished in his flesh the enmity, even the law of commandments contained in ordinances; for to make in himself of twain one new man, so making peace;

Pauline Titles	
PRISONER	Philemon
no title	1 & 2 Thes
Apostle	1 & 2 Cor, Col, Ga, 1 & 2 Tm, Eph
Servant	Phil
Servant / Apostle	Ro, Titus

PHILEMON
PRESCRIPT 1-3

Verses one through three begin the Opening, containing the prescript. The elements include the author, credentials, recipients, co-recipients and a grace and peace wish.

[1-3]
[1][π] Paul, a prisoner of Jesus Christ, and Timothy our brother, unto Philemon our dearly beloved, and fellow laborer,
[2] And to our beloved Apphia, and Archippus our fellow soldier, and to the church in thy house:
[3][π] Grace to you, and peace, from God our Father and the Lord Jesus Christ.

[1][π] The first word of every Pauline letter is the author: **Paul**. Only in this letter does he, at the start, call himself **a prisoner** (δέσμιος)(vv 9, 13). It is not of Rome nor Caesar that Paul is prisoner, but **of Christ Jesus**- the cause (Phil 1:21) for whom he is in prison and under whose authority he resides (Eph 1:21ff; Jn 19:11). The absence of the apostolic title suggests that what is to follow is personal and friendly in tone. **Timothy our brother** (Eph 3:15), serves as co-author or better co-sponsor, since he did not help in the actual writing of the letter. **Philemon** is mentioned only here in the New Testament. It is very important to keep the recipient of the letter and the relationship the writer has with the recipient in view as the letter is read. The scope and disposition displayed in the text is directly related to the addressee (e.g., Ro 1:1, **To all the saints in Rome....**). **Dearly beloved** (ἀγαπητῷ) is a common term used of the special and endearing relationships between brethren. Philemon is also a **fellow laborer** or *co-worker* (συνεργῷ) in the cause for Christ.

[2] "It is generally assumed that **Apphia** was Philemon's wife [Chrysostom], and perhaps **Archippus** was their son" (IBC). The reference to **Archippus** in Colossians has many believing that he was the pastor of this house church (in Laodicea[?]). Colossians 4:17 states, **And say to Archippus, 'Take heed to the ministry which you have received in the Lord, that you may fulfill it.'** His designation as **fellow soldier** (συστρατιώτη) is probably to be taken as metaphorical (2 Tim 2:3-4) or possibly indicates some past military service. The only other individual called such is Epaphroditus (Phil 2:25). Other house churches are referred to in Paul's epistles (Ro 16:3-5, Priscilla and Aquila; Col 4:15, Nymphas in Laodocia). "It wasn't until the third century A.D. that any record of separate church buildings can be found" (Richards).

[3][π] A **grace** and **peace** wish are customary in prescripts. Grace (χάρις) was the Greek ideal– for God to be gratuitous to one. **Peace** (εἰρήνη), the Hebrew ideal, is the idea of oneness and unity with God with all its benefits (Eph 2:14ff). The sources of bestowal: **from the Father and the Lord Jesus Christ.**

PHILEMON SKETCHED
EXORDIUM 4-7

[4-7][π]

I am giving thanks to my God always,

> *when I am remembering* you in my prayers,
> *hearing* of your love and the faith
>> *which* you have to the Lord Jesus and unto all the saints,
>> *in order that* the partnership of your faith might be effective with
>> the knowledge of every good thing which is in you unto Christ

for I had much joy and comfort at your love

> *because* the spirits of the saints have been and continue to be revived by you,
> brother.

Main clauses: BOLD, Subordinate/Coordinate elements: ITALICS

REFERENCES

[4][π]

(Eph 1:3ff) Blessed be the God and Father of our Lord Jesus Christ, who hath blessed us with all spiritual blessings in heavenly places in Christ:

[5]

(Col 1:7, 8) As you also learned of Epaphras our dear fellow servant, who is for you a faithful minister of Christ; [8] Who also declared unto us your love in the Spirit.

(Col 4:12) Epaphras, who is one of you, a servant of Christ, salutes you, always laboring fervently for you in prayers, that you may stand perfect and complete in all the will of God.

[6]

(Lk 5:10) And so was also James, and John, the sons of Zebedee, which were partners with Simon. And Jesus said unto Simon, Fear not; from henceforth thou shalt catch men.

(Col 1:9) For this cause we also, since the day we heard it, do not cease to pray for you, and to desire that you might be filled with the knowledge of his will in all wisdom and spiritual understanding;

(Phil 1:9) And this I pray, that your love may abound yet more and more in knowledge and in all judgment;

(Eph 1:5) Having predestinated us unto the adoption of children by Jesus Christ to himself, according to the good pleasure of his will....

(2 Cor 6:11-12) O Corinthians, our mouth is open unto you, our heart is enlarged. [12] You are not straitened in us, but you are straitened in your own bowels.

PHILEMON
EXORDIUM 4-7

Verses four through seven form the exordium of the letter.
It is the section preceding the main discourse.
A majority of times in Paul's letters, it begins with
thanksgiving or blessed and contains a prayer.

[4-7]
[4][π] I thank my God, making mention of you always in my prayers, [5] Hearing of your love and faith, which thou hast toward the Lord Jesus, and toward all saints; [6] That the communication of your faith may become effectual by the acknowledging of every good thing which is in you in Christ Jesus. [7] For we have great joy and consolation in your love, because the bowels of the saints are refreshed by you, brother.

[4][π] Webster's defines an exordium as "the introductory part of a discourse, treatise, etc." Often this section seeks to assure positive reception of the letter and may preview the topic. **Thanksgiving** begins eight of Paul's twelve exordiums. The use of the singular **you** in this verse and in verse seven speaks of the singular purpose of communicating to Philemon. The other recipients, as will be seen, are not in a position to act upon the specific things Paul will say to Philemon.

[5] **Hearing of....** (ἀκούων) tells of the cause and occasion for giving thanks. Epaphras and Onesimus could testify for Philemon's service (Col 1:7, 8; 4:12). The unusual order of the words (chiasm) in this verse can be taken as "hearing of your **faith** in the **Lord Jesus** and your **love** for **all the saints**" (IBC).

[6] This verse gives a purpose or end for which Paul was praying (**in my prayers... that the....**). The Old English word **communication** no longer retains the sense of the Greek. Translations vary: *sharing* (NIV), *fellowship* (NASB), and *part-nership* (NAB). The best rendering is *partnership* (κοινωνία, Lk 5:10). He prays that their common goals and efforts *might be* **effectual** or *energized* (ἐνεργὴς) *with the knowledge of every* **good thing** *which is in you unto* **Christ**. *Knowledge* (ἐπιγνώσει) is often a stated desire in the exordium section (Col 1:9; Phil 1:9). Paul believed that the Christian life is a pursuit of all that can be known of God. The last phrase can serve as a creedal formula speaking of that ultimate goal: *unto* **Christ** (εἰς Χριστόν, Eph 1:5; Ro 11:36, **For of him, and through him, and to him, are all things: to whom be glory for ever. Amen**).

[7] **For** (γὰρ) *I had* **great joy and** *comfort* or **consolation** (παράκλησιν) *at your* **love**. *I had* (ἔσχον) suggests something specific- *that* (ὅτι) or **because the bowels of the saints** *have been and continue to be* **refreshed** (Pf. Pass., ἀναπέπαυται) **by you brother** (ἀδελφέ)! To refresh means to *rest* and *revive*. **Bowels** (*inward parts*, τὰ σπλάγχνα) refer to the ancient near east seat of emotion. Children were called the 'bowels' of their parents (2 Cor 6:11-12). *Heart* or *soul* often serve as an equivalent expression.

PHILEMON SKETCHED

TOPIC 8-16

[8-9][π]

Wherefore, *although having much boldness* in Christ to order that which is suitable for you, because of love,

I chose to exhort, being such a one as Paul the elder, but now even a prisoner of Christ Jesus.

[10-16]

I am exhorting you concerning my son,

>*whom* I bore while in bonds, Onesimus who formerly to you was useless,
>>but now both to you and to me is useful,

>*whom* I sent back to you himself:
>>*this* one is my heart

>*whom* I was desiring to retain to myself,
>>*in order that* in your behalf he might serve with me in the bonds of the gospel
>*but* without your knowledge I would not do anything,
>*lest* your good might be based on constraint rather than willingly.

for perhaps because of this, he was separated to this hour,

>*in order that* you might retain him forever no longer as a slave,
>>*but rather* above a slave, a beloved brother, certainly he was to me,
>*and* how much more to you both in the flesh and in the Lord.

REFERENCES

[8][π]

(1 Cor 1:10) Now I beseech you, brethren, by the name of our Lord Jesus Christ, that ye all speak the same thing, and that there be no divisions among you; but that ye be perfectly joined together in the same mind and in the same judgment.

(I Thes 5:14) Now we exhort you, brethren, warn them that are unruly, comfort the feebleminded, support the weak, be patient toward all men.

(Eph 5:4) Neither filthiness, nor foolish talking, nor jesting, which are not convenient: but rather giving of thanks.

(Col 3:18) Wives, submit yourselves unto your own husbands, as it is fit in the Lord.

[9]

(Ro 12:1-2) I beseech you therefore, brethren, by the mercies of God, that you present your bodies a living sacrifice, holy, acceptable unto God, which is your reasonable service. [2] And be not conformed to this world: but be transformed by the renewing of your mind, that you may prove what is that good, and acceptable, and perfect, will of God.

(Lk 1:18) And Zacharias said unto the angel, Whereby shall I know this? for I am an old man, and my wife well stricken in years.

(Titus 2:2) That the aged men be sober, grave, temperate, sound in faith, in charity, in patience.

PHILEMON
TOPIC 8-16

Verses eight through sixteen form the topic of the letter. It is the primary reason for the existence of the letter. Lesser matters will be pushed into the closing section.

[8-10]

[8][π] Wherefore, although I might be much bold in Christ to enjoin thee that which is convenient,
[9] Yet for love's sake I rather beseech you, being such an one as Paul the aged, and now also a prisoner of Jesus Christ.
[10] I beseech you for my son Onesimus, whom I have begotten in my bonds:

[8][π] The topic will be exposed and discussed but the author will not yet tell Philemon how to act upon this section. The first line of the topic section is key. It often reveals not only the topic (sometimes in a disclosure formula, 1 Cor 1:10), but the author's disposition to the recipient. **Wherefore** (Διό) draws inferences from the former (vv 4-7) to this section. Nearly everything in the exordium relates to the present situation. Some refer to this as foreshadowing. **Although** (ἔχων) Paul had the authority to **enjoin** or *command* (ἐπιτάσσειν), he chose not to. Many purport that this is the only appropriate way to direct people from an authoritative position. This is simply not true. The posture and character of the recipient dictates the method (I Thes 5:14). In this letter, knowing the predisposition of Philemon and his service to others, to order would be unnecessary and inappropriate. **Convenient** (τὸ ἀνῆκον) refers to what Paul has judged to be *suitable, appropriate* and *fitting* (Eph 5:4; Col 3:18).

[9] Paul urges with "appeals of love, old age, and imprisonment...." (NIVBC). To **beseech** (παρακαλῶ) in modern Greek, means *please*. It means to *urge, beg,* and *plead* in this context (Ro 12:1-2). Lohse notes that Paul "empties himself of his rights in order to compel Philemon also to waive his rights". Some see **aged** (πρεσβύτης) as meaning ambassador (πρεσβευτής). The term, however, seems best taken as old age (Zacharias, Lk 1:18; Titus 2:2). Barclay notes that Hippocrates listed a presbutâs as one from ages 49-56. Even though Paul was called a *young man* in Acts 7:58, he would now be considered 'senior' or *elder*.

[10] "Waiving his right to make demands on Philemon, as the prisoner of Christ he prefers entreaty, appealing as a father for his own **son** whom with consummate tact he now mentions for the first time" (Bruce). **Son** (τέκνου) speaks of Paul being the instrument of Onesimus' salvation. The event of new birth occurred when Paul was **in bonds**, i.e., imprisoned. Unfortunately, we are left to imagine how this runaway slave from the Lycus Valley crossed the path of the Apostle Paul in Rome. With an estimated 1:1 slave to citizen ratio, Rome was a good place for a run away slave to get lost in the crowds.

REFERENCES

[11]

(Acts 7:58) And cast him out of the city, and stoned him: and the witnesses laid down their clothes at a young man's feet, whose name was Saul.

(2 Cor 5:17) Therefore if any man be in Christ, he is a new creature: old things are passed away; behold, all things are become new.

[12]

(Col 4:7-9) All my state shall Tychicus declare unto you, who is a beloved brother, and a faithful minister and fellowservant in the Lord: [8] Whom I have sent unto you for the same purpose, that he might know your estate, and comfort your hearts; [9] With Onesimus, a faithful and beloved brother, who is one of you. They shall make known unto you all things which are done here.

[13]

(2 Tm 4:9-12) Do thy diligence to come shortly unto me: [10] For Demas hath forsaken me, having loved this present world, and is departed unto Thessalonica; Crescens to Galatia, Titus unto Dalmatia. [11] Only Luke is with me. Take Mark, and bring him with thee: for he is profitable to me for the ministry. [12] And Tychicus have I sent to Ephesus.

(Ac 28:30-31) And Paul dwelt two whole years in his own hired house, and received all that came in unto him, [31] Preaching the kingdom of God, and teaching those things which concern the Lord Jesus Christ, with all confidence, no man forbidding him.

[14]

(2 Cor 9:7) Every man according as he purposeth in his heart, so let him give; not grudgingly, or of necessity: for God loveth a cheerful giver.

(1 Pet 5:2) Feed the flock of God which is among you, taking the oversight thereof, not by constraint, but willingly; not for filthy lucre, but of a ready mind;

(Phil 2:17) Yea, and if I be offered upon the sacrifice and service of your faith, I joy, and rejoice with you all.

[15]

(Ro 5:7) For scarcely for a righteous man will one die: yet peradventure for a good man some would even dare to die.

[11-16]
[11] Which in time past was to thee unprofitable, but now profitable to thee and to me:
[12] Whom I have sent again: thou therefore receive him, that is, mine own bowels:
[13] Whom I would have retained with me, that in thy stead he might have ministered unto me in the bonds of the gospel:
[14] But without thy mind would I do nothing; that thy benefit should not be as it were of necessity, but willingly.
[15] For perhaps he therefore departed for a season, that thou shouldest receive him for ever;
[16] Not now as a servant, but above a servant, a brother beloved, specially to me, but how much more unto thee, both in the flesh, and in the Lord?

[11] Verses 10-13 are about Onesimus (**whom... which... whom... whom....**). Since Onesimus' name means 'profitable', there is a subtle word play– *who formerly to you was useless* (ἄ/χρηστον), *but now to you and to me is useful* (εὔ/χρηστον). Onesimus has now become Onesimus (2 Cor 5:17). In the ancient world, slaves could be very **profitable**. They took part in every part of the economy: scribes, lawyers, etc. Our western notion of slavery does not compare well with the ancient near east cultures.

[12] **Whom I have sent** *back to you himself* identifies the courier and the situation (Col 4:7-9). "Onesimus must have become very dear to Paul in these months in prison, for he pays him the great tribute of saying that to send him to Philemon is like sending a bit of his heart (lit., *this one is my* **bowels** [v 7])" (Barclay). An important facet of Paul's ministry life is displayed in this verse. Note 2 Cor 12:15a, **But I will most gladly spend [myself] and be utterly spent for your souls** (Amp). Ministry is an investment of self into the lives of others.

[13] Many served with Paul during his imprisonment. It was unusual even when free, for him to work alone (2 Tm 4:9-12). Was Paul suggesting an arrangement in this verse: *in order that IN YOUR BEHALF he might serve...*? Philemon had the authority to make Onesimus serve with Paul. **In the Lord**, the insubordinate slave has become a voluntary servant (διακονῇ). **In the bonds of the gospel** (εὐαγγελίου) tells of the difficult, ongoing work while in prison (Ac 28:30-31).

[14] Paul, even as an Apostle, did not have a legal or ethical privilege to **retain** Onesimus without Philemon's *knowledge* (**mind**, γνώμης). Paul did not do what he wanted, but rather what he should do. Even though there was much *good* (τὸ ἀγαθόν) or **benefit** happening, it was without Philemon's consent and knowledge. Ministerial ethics must be observed. **Willingly** (ἑκούσιον) is the proper attitude accompanying obedience (2 Cor 9:7; 1 Pet 5:2; Phil 2:17).

[15] **For perhaps** (τάχα, Ro 5:7) introduces a suggestion that this temporary situation may work out to a far better permanent one. It has been noted that this is a "delicate way of putting it": *he was separated to this hour* [departed] (ἐχωρίσθη, divine passive?). In his persuasion, Paul was softening the assessment of the events.

[16] *No longer as a slave* (δοῦλον) falls short of telling Philemon to free Onesimus. His relationship has been elevated, but his position unchanged. "In the order of nature [**in the flesh**] and in the order of grace [**in the Lord**]" (Zerwick), Philemon now has a **beloved brother**. Onesimus comes with an assessment from Paul: he *absolutely* (μάλιστα) *was* a beloved brother to me.

PHILEMON SKETCHED

PARENESIS 17-21

[17][π]

If therefore, you have me as a partner,
receive him as me.

[18]

And if he wronged you
or is owing anything,
charge this to me.

[19]

I Paul write with my hand,

I shall repay,
not to mention that even yourself you are owing to me.

[20]

Yes, brother, may I benefit from you in the Lord,

relieve my soul in Christ.

[21]

Having been and continuing to be confident at your obedience,
I wrote to you,
knowing that even above that which I am saying, you shall do.

Main clauses: BOLD, Subordinate/Coordinate elements: ITALICS

REFERENCES

[17][π]
(Eph 4:1) I therefore, the prisoner of the Lord, beseech you that you walk worthy of the vocation wherewith you are called,
(Col 3:1) If you then be risen with Christ, seek those things which are above, where Christ sitteth on the right hand of God.
(Phil 2:1-2) If there be therefore any consolation in Christ, if any comfort of love, if any fellowship of the Spirit, if any bowels and mercies, [2] Fulfil ye my joy, that you be likeminded, having the same love, being of one accord, of one mind.
(Lk 5:10) And so was also James, and John, the sons of Zebedee, which were partners with Simon. And Jesus said unto Simon, Fear not; from henceforth thou shalt catch men.
[18]
(Ro 5:13) For until the law sin was in the world: but sin is not imputed when there is no law.
[19]
(Ro 16:22) I Tertius, who wrote this epistle, salute you in the Lord.
(Gal 6:11) You see how large a letter I have written unto you with mine own hand.
(Col 4:18) The salutation by the hand of me Paul. Remember my bonds. Grace be with you. Amen.
(1 Cor 16:21) The salutation of me Paul with mine own hand.
(2 Thes 3:17) The salutation of Paul with mine own hand, which is the token in every epistle: so I write.

PHILEMON
PARENESIS 17-19

*Verses seventeen through twenty-one form the parenesis of
the letter. Paul now exhorts Philemon, via directives,
to act upon the issue in the topic section.
The connection, if any at all, of the topic section
and the parenetic must be carefully validated.*

[17–19]
[17][π] If you count
me therefore a
partner, receive him
as myself.
[18] If he has
wronged thee, or
owes thee ought,
put that on mine
account;
[19] I Paul have
written it with mine
own hand, I will
repay it: albeit I do
not say to thee how
thou owest unto
me even thine own
self besides.

[17][π] Three imperatives are issued: **receive him** (v 17), *bill*
me (v 18), and **refresh** me (v 20). The word **therefore** (οὖν) is
often found bridging the topic section and actions prescribed
(Eph 4:1; Col 3:1). Paul did not just discuss the topic, he calls
for action upon it. Although **if** (Εἰ) could be translated *since*,
the directive **receive him** teeters on the condition **if** we are
partners (Phil 2:1-2). The partnership (Lk 5:10, **James, and
John, the sons of Zebedee, which were partners with Simon**)
shared by the two is the basis for Onesimus' reception. As you
would receive me, **receive him**. Typically, a captured Roman
slave would at least be flogged and possibly killed.

[18] Did Paul know all the details of Onesimus' departure?
Why would he say **if he has wronged thee**? The general term
wronged (ἠδίκησέν) should not be overlooked. Paul was wise
enough to know that he had only heard Onesimus' view of
the details. To **put on mine account** (ἐλλόγα) is "an
accountant's term", as in "debit me" (Ro 5:13). It is commonly
held that "like many runaway slaves, Onesimus financed his
flight by stealing something of value from his master"
(Richards). Of note is that his absence is itself theft– his
absence of service. Paul intercedes in behalf of his loss. It is in
these verses that substitutionary themes surface.

[19] Lightfoot notes that "The introduction of his own name
[ἐγὼ Παῦλος] gives it the character of a formal and binding
signature" (cheiro-graphon?). We know that Paul did not
physically write all of his epistles; **I Tertius who wrote this
epistle, salute you in the Lord** (Ro 16:22). It appears that he
usually used an amanuensis: "one whose employment is to
write what another dictates" (Webster's). It is noteworthy
when he does write for himself; **You see how large a letter I
have written unto you with mine own hand** (Gal 6:11; Col
4:18; [v 21]). Some letters suggest Paul took over writing at the
final salutations (1 Cor 16:21; 2 Thes 3:17). **Mine own hand** is
a customary way of offering a "promissory note"- a common
practice throughout history.

REFERENCES

[19]

(Ro 5:19) For as by one man's disobedience many were made sinners, so by the obedience of one shall many be made righteous.

(Gal 1:4) Who gave himself for our sins, that he might deliver us from this present evil world, according to the will of God and our Father:

(1 Tim 6:2) And they that have believing masters, let them not despise them, because they are brethren; but rather do them service, because they are faithful and beloved, partakers of the benefit. These things teach and exhort.

[20][π]

(Lk 12:19) And I will say to my soul, Soul, thou hast much goods laid up for many years; take thine ease, eat, drink, and be merry.

(Mt 11:28-30) Come unto me, all you that labor and are heavy laden, and I will give you rest. [29] Take my yoke upon you, and learn of me; for I am meek and lowly in heart: and you shall find rest unto your souls. [30] For my yoke is easy, and my burden is light.

[19] I Paul have written it with mine own hand, I will repay it: albeit I do not say to you how thou owest unto me even thine own self besides.
[20][π] Yea, brother, let me have joy of thee in the Lord: refresh my bowels in the Lord.
[21] Having confidence in thy obedience I wrote unto thee, knowing that thou wilt also do more than I say.

The intercession in these verses is often taught about Christ in Paul's epistles (Ro 5:19; Gal 1:4: 1 Tim 6:2). The second clause (owest unto me thine own self) suggests Paul as the instrument of Philemon's conversion as well. "In Paul's view, Philemon's spiritual indebtedness to him should easily cover all of Onesimus' wrongdoing" (NIVBC). These verses clearly define the letter as a letter of intercession and commendation.

[20][π] **Brother** (ἀδελφέ), another personal touch of friendship, occurs for the third time (vv 2, 7). Before the last directive, Paul motivates on a particularly personal note: **let me have joy of thee in the Lord** (opt., ὀναίμην). **In the Lord** reveals the unselfishness of the request. **Refresh** *my inward parts in Christ* (ἀνάπαυσόν)(Lk 12:19, **take thine ease**; Mt 11:28-30, **I shall give you rest**) means to relieve of the anxiety and stress of this situation. Paul truly loved Onesimus. Philemon, who was commended for this very thing (v 7), is asked to do this for Paul.

[21] A vote of **confidence** closes this section: *having been and continuing to be confident at your* **obedience**.... How can Paul speak of obedience (ὑπακοῇ) when he has not commanded Philemon (vv 8-9)? Although Paul has not used his rightful authority, he has compelled Philemon toward two options: receive him or send him for my use. Paul more than suspects (**knowing**) that Philemon *will do above* (ὑπὲρ) *that which* he says. Paul tactfully opened the floodgates of persuasion upon Philemon for Onesimus, for himself, and for the work of Christ.

Distribution of Commands		
OPENING	Prescript	0
	Exordium	0
BODY	Topic	0
	Parenesis	3
CLOSING	Postscript	1

We see here one of the earliest examples of the mode in which Christianity operated upon these relations; not by any violent disruption of the organisation of society, such as could only have produced another Servile War, but by gradually leavening and interpenetrating society with the spirit of a religion which recognised the equality of all men in the sight of God. Conbeare & Howson

PHILEMON SKETCHED
POST SCRIPT 22-25

[22]

Now, at the same time also, prepare a lodging for me.

For I hope that by means of your prayers, I shall be given to you.

[23-24]

Epaphras, greets you: my fellow prisoner in Christ Jesus, Mark, Aristarchus, Demas, Luke, my co-workers.

[25]

The grace of the Lord Jesus Christ be with your spirit.

REFERENCES

[22][π]

(Ac 28:23) And when they had appointed him a day, there came many to him into his lodging; to whom he expounded and testified the kingdom of God, persuading them concerning Jesus, both out of the law of Moses, and out of the prophets, from morning till evening.

(Ro 12:13) Distributing to the necessity of saints; given to hospitality.

(Ro 15:24) Whensoever I take my journey into Spain, I will come to you: for I trust to see you in my journey, and to be brought on my way thitherward by you, if first I be somewhat filled with your company.

[23][π]

(Col 1:7) As you also learned of Epaphras our dear fellow servant, who is for you a faithful minister of Christ;

(Col 4:12, 13) Epaphras, who is one of you, a servant of Christ, salutes you, always laboring fervently for you in prayers, that ye may stand perfect and complete in all the will of God. [13] For I bear him record, that he hath a great zeal for you, and them that are in Laodicea, and them in Hierapolis.

[24]

(Col 4:10-11) Aristarchus my fellow prisoner salutes you, and Marcus, sister's son to Barnabas, (touching whom you received commandments: if he come unto you, receive him;) [11] And Jesus, which is called Justus, who are of the circumcision. These only are my fellow workers unto the kingdom of God, which have been a comfort unto me.

(2 Tim 4:11) Only Luke is with me. Take Mark, and bring him with thee: for he is profitable to me for the ministry.

(Acts 19:29) And the whole city was filled with confusion: and having caught Gaius and Aristarchus, men of Macedonia, Paul's companions in travel, they rushed with one accord into the theatre.

(Acts 20:4) And there accompanied him into Asia Sopater of Berea; and of the Thessalonians, Aristarchus and Secundus; and Gaius of Derbe, and Timothy....

(Acts 27:2) And entering into a ship of Adramyttium, we launched, meaning to sail by the coasts of Asia; one Aristarchus, a Macedonian of Thessalonica, being with us.

(Col 4:14) Luke, the beloved physician, and Demas, greet you.

(Phil 2:4) Look not every man on his own things, but every man also on the things of others.

(2 Tim 4:10) For Demas hath forsaken me, having loved this present world, and is departed unto Thessalonica; Crescens to Galatia, Titus unto Dalmatia.

PHILEMON
CLOSING 22-25

Verses twenty-two through twenty-five form the closing of the letter in the form of a post-script. Paul gives only a few elements in this letter as compared to his other letters.

[22-25]
[22][π] But withal prepare me also a lodging: for I trust that through your prayers I shall be given unto you.
[23][π] There salute thee Epaphras, my fellow prisoner in Christ Jesus;
[24] Mark, Aristarchus, Demas, Luke, my fellowlabourers.
[25][π] The grace of our Lord Jesus Christ be with your spirit. Amen.

[22][π] **But** (δὲ) or *now*, is often a particle that starts a new section. Unfortunately, this word often goes untranslated [!?]. **Withal** (ἅμα) or *at the same time*. A **lodging** (ξενίαν, Ac 28:23) was a part of Philemon's service as co-worker and partner (Ro 12:13). His means for this service suggest he is wealthy. Paul hoped or trusted that God's will would be moved by the **prayers** of this church (**your** is plural here) and he would **be given** (χαρισθήσομαι, divine passive) **unto** them. Many believe that Paul was released from Rome and went on a fourth missionary journey (Ro 15:24).

[23][π] **Salute** or *greets*. **Epaphras** was a servant from the Colossian church who had a burden for Laodicea and Hierapolis (Col 1:7, 4:12, 13). **Fellow prisoner** "perhaps means only that Epaphras voluntarily shared Paul's imprisonment at Rome by taking up residence with him...." (C&H). A comparison of greetings in Colossians suggests a number of connections to time, place, and possibly Tychicus. These issues fall outside the scope and purpose of this text.

[24] **Mark** "the cousin of Barnabas" is also known as John-Mark (Acts 13:5-13, 15:36-40; Col 4:10-11; 2 Tim 4:11, **profitable to me for the ministry**). According to Papias of Heirapolis (A.D. 130), Mark ministered with Peter in Rome serving as "interpreter" and compiling his teaching about Jesus' life (WWB). **Aristarchus** was ('best ruler') (Acts 19:29, 20:4, 27:2; Col 4:10) "one of Paul's most constant and faithful 'co-workers'". He was a travel companion who had endured the riot at Ephesus. It is of note in relation to the Rome/Caesarea debate that he sails for Rome with Paul (27:2). **Demas** has not yet made his critical fall (Col 4:14; Phil 2:4; 2 Tim 4:10). **Luke** the physician was with Paul during the "we passages" in Acts (16:10-17, 20:5-21:18, 27:1-28:16).

	Philemon	Colossians
v 2	Archippus	4:17
v 23	Epaphras	4:14
v 24	Mark	4:10
v 24	Aristarchus	4:10
v 24	Demas	4:14
v 24	Luke	4:14

[25][π] As was his custom, Paul ended with a **grace** wish. **Amen** has dubious manuscript support. Many manuscripts also include some form of "from Rome".

CHAPTER FIVE

A THIEF IN THE NIGHT: 1 THESSALONIANS

BACKGROUND
ACTS 17:1-16

On Paul's second missionary journey, we find the difficulties and victories of spreading the gospel among the Gentile peoples. Paul, having parted from Barnabas (15:36-41), goes through Syria and Cilicia. After Derbe, he finds Timothy in Lystra (16:1ff) and takes him along. Phrygia and Galatia were next on the list. In an intriguing verse (16:6), we find the Holy Spirit forbidding them to **preach the word in Asia** (mod. Turkey). Spirit leading is normative of the Christian walk, Ro 8:14, **For as many as are led by the Spirit of God, these are sons of God**. When they come to Mysia, they attempt to go to Bythinia (NE) but were not allowed by the Spirit. They then settle in at Troas (16:8) where Paul's sees the "vision" (ὅραμα) of the Macedonian man calling for help (16:9). Paul enters Europe by water, staying at Samothracia one night and then on to Neopolis. His party then moves to Philippi, where on the sabbath, they meet Lydia (16:11-15). After Philippi, Paul continues to Thessalonica.

[17:1]

[1] Now when they had passed through Amphipolis and Apol-lonia, they came to Thessalonica, where was a synagogue of the Jews.

[1] Paul **passed through Amphipolis and Apollonia** for unknown reasons. Some suggest the absence of a synagogue. **Thessalonica** (modern Saloniki) provides a fascinating example of what a Roman city could be like. It was a "free city" in the empire -thus granting it self-rule. Unlike Jerusalem, no soldiers were stationed to guard it. It was the capital city of four districts of Macedonia. The original name of the city was Therma, but Casander (king of Macedonia, 315 BC), renamed it after his wife, the sister of Alexander the Great. Geographically, Thessalonica was unrivaled. Located next to a natural harbor on the east side of Greece and sitting on the Via Egnatia, Thessalonica seemed destined to be a prominent city. With the world ruled by Rome, Thessalonica was a gateway to the East. Only two other cities could compare in the trade of the day: Ephesus and Corinth. The existence of a **synagogue** indicates at least a small Jewish community. Considering the events that occur, it is reasonable to assume a significant Jewish group was present.

REFERENCES

[3]
(Lk 24:32) And they said one to another, Did not our heart burn within us, while he talked with us by the way, and while he opened to us the scriptures?
(Lk 24:45) Then opened he their understanding, that they might understand the scriptures,
(Ac 3:18) But those things, which God before had showed by the mouth of all his prophets, that Christ should suffer, he hath so fulfilled.

49-52 AD	Second Journey	Ac 15:36- 18:22	(Syria, Cilicia)
			Derbe, Lystra
			(Phrygia, Galatia)
	Macedonian Vision,		Mysia
	the Gospel Enters Europe		Troas
		→	Samothrace
			Neapolis
			Philippi
	Brief Visit, Church Established,		Amphipolis
	Jason Assaulted in Riot		Appolonia
		→	THESSALONICA
	Timothy Reports to Paul in Athens,		Berea
	Thessalonian Letters Follow		Athens
		→	Corinth

[2] And Paul, as his manner was went in unto them, and three sabbath days reasoned with them out of the scriptures,
[3] Opening and alleging that Christ must needs have suffered and risen again from the dead; and that this Jesus, whom I preach unto you, is Christ.
[4] And some of them believed and consorted with Paul and Silas; and of the devout Greeks a great multitude, and of the chief women not a few.
[5] But the Jews who believed not, moved with envy, took unto them certain vile fellows of the baser sort, and gathered a company, and set all the city in an uproar, and assaulted the house of Jason, and sought to bring them out to the people.
[6] And when they found them not, they drew Jason and certain brethren unto the rulers of the city, crying, These that have turned the world upside down are come here also,

[2] Paul's **manner** or *custom* (εἰωθὸς) was to utilize the forum of the synagogue to preach Christ. Having been a Pharisee, he would know the protocols, what to say, and have the advantage of speaking to people who were read in the prophetic scriptures fulfilled by Christ. His stay lasts **three sabbath days** (3-4 weeks). He **reasoned** (διελέξατο) or proclaimed argumentatively **out of** (ἀπὸ) **the scriptures**. Robertson states, "Paul appealed to the scriptures as text and basis of his ideas". The scriptures at this time, of course, was the Old Testament.

[3] The manner of his reasoning (v 2) was by **opening and alleging**. In **opening** (διανοίγων), he sought "to explain something which has been previously hidden or obscure" (Bruce)(Lk 24:32, 45). In **alleging** (παρατιθέμενος), he was advancing argumentation- the setting forth of reasons together with the conclusions drawn from them. The content of Paul's message: literally, **the Christ**. This would include the necessity of his crucifixion (Ac 3:18), his resurrection, and his identification as the Christ: *this one is the Christ.*

> Paul appealed to the scriptures as text
> and basis of his ideas. Robertson

[4] The gospel is **believed by some**. They **consort** (προσεκληρώθησαν) or *put their lot in* with Paul and Silas. The term **devout** (σεβομένων) means those having a reverence for God or "God-fearers". Their presence as Greeks at the synagogue suggests they may have been proselytes or reverent observers. **Chief women** may be understood as *prominent women* (τῶν πρώτων).

[5] The **Jews** become jealous, probably because of the following Paul takes from them. Success naturally breads envy. They conspire in accord with their character.

[6] **They drew** or *they were dragging* Jason and others abiding with him. The **rulers of the city** are the *politarchs* (πολιτάρχας) which ruled the city, independent of the Roman magistrates. The content of their persecution is simplistic (vv 6b-7); the trouble makers who appose Caesar are here! The phrase **turned the world upside down** (ἀναστατώσαντες), taken as an unintended compliment, indicates those who *disrupt* the present order (i.e., **the world**). It is used in Gal. 5:12 of the Judaisers who disrupted the walk of the Galatian churches, **I would they were even cut off who *trouble* you.**

REFERENCES

[7-8]

(Jn 19:12) And from thenceforth Pilate sought to release him: but the Jews cried out, saying, If thou let this man go, thou art not Caesar's friend: whosoever makes himself a king speaks against Caesar.

[10]

(Ac 17:1-3) Now when they had passed through Amphipolis and Apollonia, they came to Thessalonica, where was a synagogue of the Jews: [2] And Paul, as his manner was, went in unto them, and three sabbath days reasoned with them out of the scriptures, [3] Opening and alleging, that Christ must needs have suffered, and risen again from the dead; and that this Jesus, whom I preach unto you, is Christ.

[11]

(1 Pet 5:2) Feed the flock of God which is among you, taking the oversight thereof, not by constraint, but willingly; not for filthy lucre, but of a ready mind;

(Ac 4:9) If we this day be examined of the good deed done to the impotent man, by what means he is made whole;

(Ac 12:19) And when Herod had sought for him, and found him not, he examined the keepers, and commanded that they should be put to death. And he went down from Judea to Caesarea, and there abode.

[13]

(1 Thes 2:14-16) For you, brethren, became followers of the churches of God which in Judea are in Christ Jesus: for ye also have suffered like things of your own countrymen, even as they have of the Jews: [15] Who both killed the Lord Jesus, and their own prophets, and have persecuted us; and they please not God, and are contrary to all men: [16] Forbidding us to speak to the Gentiles that they might be saved, to fill up their sins alway: for the wrath is come upon them to the uttermost.

(2 Tim 4:9-11) Do thy diligence to come shortly unto me: [10] For Demas hath forsaken me, having loved this present world, and is departed unto Thessalonica; Crescens to Galatia, Titus unto Dalmatia. [11] Only Luke is with me. Take Mark, and bring him with thee: for he is profitable to me for the ministry.

[7] Whom Jason hath received; and these all do contrary to the decrees of Caesar, saying that there is another king, one Jesus.
[8] And they troubled the people and the rulers of the city, when they heard these things.
[9] And when they had taken security of Jason, and of the others, they let them go.
[10] And the brethren immediately sent away Paul and Silas by night unto Berea, who, coming there, went into the synagogue of the Jews.
[11] These were more noble than those in Thessalonica, in that they received the word with all readiness of mind, and searched the scriptures daily, whether those things were so.
[12] Therefore, many of them believed; also of honorable women who were Greeks, and of men, not a few.
[13] But when the Jews of Thessalonica had knowledge that the word of God was preached by Paul at Berea, they came there also, and stirred up the people.
[14] And then immediately the brethren sent away Paul to go as it were to the sea; but Silas and Timothy abode there still.
[15] And they that conducted Paul brought him unto Athens; and receiving a commandment unto Silas and Timothy to come to him with all speed, they departed.
[16] Now when Paul waited for them at Athens,....

[7-8] Although understanding the kingship of Christ as preached by Paul (v 3), the slanderous and cunning accusation that Jesus somehow threatened the throne of Caesar is without foundation. The Jews manufactured this accusation which is similar to what was said of Jesus in Jerusalem. **And the whole multitude of them arose, and led him unto Pilate. And they began to accuse him, saying, We found this fellow perverting the nation, and forbidding to give tribute to Caesar, saying that he himself is Christ a King** (Lk 23:1-2)(Jn 19:12).

[9] The **security** (τὸ ἱκανὸν) taken may be similar to our idea of a bond. Some believe that it served as payment for a future trial. Others see it as confiscated to ensure the peace.

[10] Paul's *modus operandi* has not changed from Thessalonica (Ac 17:1-3).

[11] The first sentence of this verse can be more precisely translated. The idea of **more noble than** (εὐγενέστεροι) does not indicate more virtuous. It speaks of those who are of higher nobility by birth. **In that** is better translated *which ones* (οἵτινες) *received* the word... **Readiness** (προθυμίας, 1 Pet 5:2) far exceeds willingness. Their readiness is demonstrated in their daily search of the scriptures. To **search** (ἀνακρίνοντες) means "to sift up and down, make careful and exact research as in legal processes as in Acts 4:9; 12:19, etc." (Robertson). **Whether those things were so** or *if it might have these things thus*. No substitute exists for finding and maintaining the truth like searching the scriptures and comparing them to all proposed doctrine, practice and worship.

[12] Because of their search for the truth, comparing Paul's understanding with the scriptures, **many of them believed**.

It is impossible to overstress
the importance of the arrival
of Christianity in Thessalonica. Barclay

[13ff] The **Jews of Thessalonica** pursue Paul and are later cited for their actions (1 Thes 2:14-16). Retaining the cohesiveness of the ministry team always seems very important (2 Tim 4:9-11).

SCHEMA OF
1 THESSALONIANS

OPENING	BODY	CLOSING

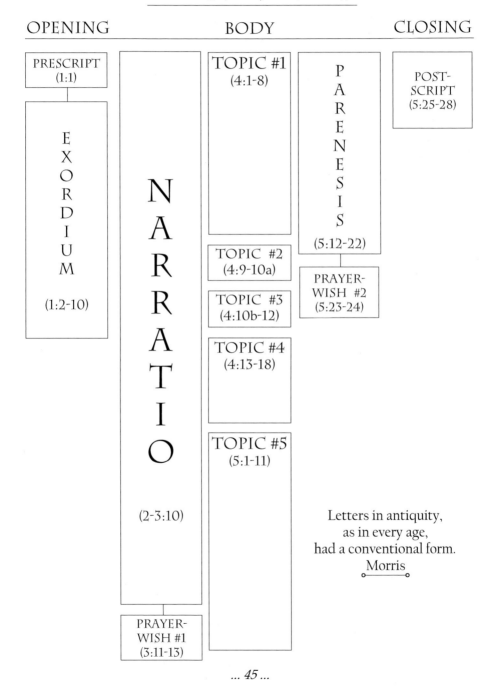

PRESCRIPT
(1:1)

E
X
O
R
D
I
U
M

(1:2-10)

N
A
R
R
A
T
I
O

(2-3:10)

PRAYER-
WISH #1
(3:11-13)

TOPIC #1
(4:1-8)

TOPIC #2
(4:9-10a)

TOPIC #3
(4:10b-12)

TOPIC #4
(4:13-18)

TOPIC #5
(5:1-11)

P
A
R
E
N
E
S
I
S

(5:12-22)

PRAYER-
WISH #2
(5:23-24)

POST-
SCRIPT
(5:25-28)

Letters in antiquity,
as in every age,
had a conventional form.
Morris

GREEK TEXT

[1][π] Παῦλος καὶ Σιλουανὸς καὶ Τιμόθεος τῇ ἐκκλησίᾳ Θεσσαλονικέων ἐν θεῷ πατρὶ καὶ κυρίῳ Ἰησοῦ Χριστῷ· χάρις ὑμῖν καὶ εἰρήνη.

[2][π] Εὐχαριστοῦμεν τῷ θεῷ πάντοτε περὶ πάντων ὑμῶν, μνείαν ποιούμενοι ἐπὶ τῶν προσευχῶν ἡμῶν, ἀδιαλείπτως [3] μνημονεύοντες ὑμῶν τοῦ ἔργου τῆς πίστεως καὶ τοῦ κόπου τῆς ἀγάπης καὶ τῆς ὑπομονῆς τῆς ἐλπίδος τοῦ κυρίου ἡμῶν Ἰησοῦ Χριστοῦ ἔμπροσθεν τοῦ θεοῦ καὶ πατρὸς ἡμῶν,

REFERENCES

[1]
(Ac 16:38) And the sergeants told these words unto the magistrates: and they feared, when they heard that they were Romans.
[2]
(1 Cor 1:4-5) I thank my God always on your behalf, for the grace of God which is given you by Jesus Christ; [5] That in every thing you are enriched by him, in all utterance, and in all knowledge
[3]
(Jm 2:26) For as the body without the spirit is dead, so faith without works is dead also.

TYPICAL OPENING ELEMENTS

PRESCRIPT:
-author
-credentials
-cosponsor(s)
-addressee(s)
-greeting(s)
-grace/peace wish
-liturgical element

EXORDIUM:
-thanksgiving
-"Blessed be..."
-favorable remembrance
-prayer

1 THESSALONIANS 1:1-3

*Chapter one forms the opening of the letter.
As in all of Paul's letters, it begins with the prescript.
The elements in the prescript include the author,
cosponsors, addressee and a grace/peace wish.*

[1-3]
[1][π] Paul, and Silvanus, and Timothy, unto the church of the Thessalonians which is in God, the Father, and in the Lord Jesus Christ: Grace be unto you, and peace, from God, our father, and the Lord Jesus Christ. [2][π] We give thanks to God always for you all, making mention of you in our prayers, [3] Remembering without ceasing your work of faith, and labor of love, and patience of hope in our Lord Jesus Christ, in the sight of God and our father,

[1][π] **Paul** is the author as indicated by the first word (Παῦλος) and first person (I) found throughout the letter. **Silvanus** and **Timothy** are cosponsors and members of Paul's mission team. Most agree that Silvanus is the Silas of Ac 15:22ff. If so, he was a leading man in the church at Jerusalem, and a Roman (Ac 16:38). Timothy, whose return occasioned this letter (3:6ff), was one of Paul's most trusted assistants. The word **church** (ἐκκλησία) is a secular term specialized "to designate a company of believers in Jesus" (Bruce). **Church** is singular here, limiting the correspondence to the newly formed congregation. Of the **grace/peace** wish, Lightfoot notes, "χάρις (**grace**) is the source of all real spiritual blessing, εἰρήνη (**peace**) their end and issue". Paul unites the Hebrew virtue (peace) and the Greek virtue (grace). Perhaps Paul derived this from Num 6:24-26, **The LORD bless you... and be gracious to you... and give you peace.**

*Verses two through ten form the exordium of the letter.
This section usually contains thanksgiving and prayer.
In form, the exordium often resembles a run-on sentence:
one long sentence with many fused together clauses.
Twelve of Paul's thirteen letters contain an exordium.*

[2][π] It is widely held that an exordium would be designed to gain a favorable disposition from the reader to encourage the reception of the letter. Its contents are positive and seem to target building the bond between the writer and readers. At times, the topics of the letter are hinted at (1 Cor 1:4-5). A multiplicity of topics can occur in the exordium. It is easy to get lost in this section and forget its place in the letter.
[3] **Without ceasing** indicates they remembered *constantly* and *unfailingly*. The content of their memory exposes the "triad of virtues": **faith, love,** and **hope.** "Paul writes of the work which results from faith, the labor which results from love and the steadfastness which results from hope" (Marshall). Truly the Thessalonian believers had an dynamic faith (Jm 2:26).

GREEK TEXT

[4] εἰδότες, ἀδελφοὶ ἠγαπημένοι ὑπὸ [τοῦ] θεοῦ, τὴν ἐκλογὴν ὑμῶν, [5] ὅτι εὐαγγέλιον ἡμῶν οὐκ ἐγενήθη εἰς ὑμᾶς ἐν λόγῳ μόνον ἀλλὰ καὶ ἐν δυνάμει καὶ ἐν πνεύματι ἁγίῳ καὶ |omit| [UBS, ἐν] πληροφορίᾳ πολλῇ, καθὼς οἴδατε οἷοι ἐγενήθημεν |omit| [UBS, ἐν] ὑμῖν δι' ὑμᾶς. [6] καὶ ὑμεῖς μιμηταὶ ἡμῶν ἐγενήθητε καὶ τοῦ κυρίου, δεξάμενοι τὸν λόγον ἐν θλίψει πολλῇ μετὰ χαρᾶς πνεύματος ἁγίου, [7] ὥστε γενέσθαι ὑμᾶς τύπον πᾶσιν τοῖς πιστεύουσιν ἐν τῇ Μακεδονίᾳ καὶ ἐν τῇ Ἀχαΐᾳ. [8] ἀφ' ὑμῶν γὰρ ἐξήχηται ὁ λόγος τοῦ κυρίου οὐ μόνον ἐν τῇ Μακεδονίᾳ καὶ |omit| [UBS, ἐν τῇ] Ἀχαΐᾳ, ἀλλ' ἐν παντὶ τόπῳ ἡ πίστις ὑμῶν ἡ πρὸς τὸν θεὸν ἐξελήλυθεν, ὥστε μὴ χρείαν ἔχειν ἡμᾶς λαλεῖν τι·

REFERENCES

[4]
(Mt 22:1-14) And Jesus answered and spake unto them again by parables, and said, [2] The kingdom of heaven is like unto a certain king, which made a marriage for his son, [3] And sent forth his servants to call them that were bidden to the wedding: and they would not come. [4] Again, he sent forth other servants, saying, Tell them which are bidden, Behold, I have prepared my dinner: my oxen and my fatlings are killed, and all things are ready: come unto the marriage. [5] But they made light of it... The wedding is ready, but they which were bidden were not worthy. [9] Go therefore into the highways, and as many as ye shall find, bid to the marriage. [10] So those servants went out into the highways, and gathered together all as many as they found, both bad and good: and the wedding was furnished with guests. [11] And when the king came in to see the guests, he saw there a man which had not on a wedding garment: [12] And he saith unto him, Friend, how camest thou in hither not having a wedding garment? And he was speechless. [13] Then said the king to the servants, Bind him hand and foot, and take him away, and cast him into outer darkness, there shall be weeping and gnashing of teeth. [14] For many are called, but few are chosen.
[5]
(Isa 40:9) O Zion, that bringest good tidings, get thee up into the high mountain; O Jerusalem, that bringest good tidings, lift up thy voice with strength; lift it up, be not afraid; say unto the cities of Judah, Behold your God!
(Isa 52:7) How beautiful upon the mountains are the feet of him that bringeth good tidings, that publisheth peace; that bringeth good tidings of good, that publisheth salvation; that saith unto Zion, Thy God reigneth!
(Lk 4:17-19) And there was delivered unto him the book of the prophet Esaias. And when he had opened the book, he found the place where it was written, [18] The Spirit of the Lord is upon me, because he hath anointed me to preach the gospel to the poor; he hath sent me to heal the broken-hearted, to preach deliverance to the captives, and recovering of sight to the blind, to set at liberty them that are bruised, [19] To preach the acceptable year of the Lord.
(1 Cor 15:1-4) Moreover, brethren, I declare unto you the gospel which I preached unto you, which also you have received, and wherein you stand; [2] By which also you are saved, if you keep in memory what I preached unto you, unless ye have believed in vain. [3] For I delivered unto you first of all that which I also received, how that Christ died for our sins according to the scriptures; [4] And that he was buried, and that he rose again the third day according to the scriptures:

[1:4-8]
[4] Knowing, Brethren beloved, your election of God.
[5] For our gospel came not unto you in word only, but also in power, and in the Holy Spirit, and in much assurance, as you know what manner of men we were among you for your sake.
[6] As you became followers of us, and of the Lord, having received the word in much affliction, with joy of the Holy Spirit,
[7] So that you were an example to all that believe in Macedonia and Achaia.
[8] For from you sounded out the word of the Lord not only in Macedonia and Achaia, but also in every place your faith toward God is spread abroad, so that we need not to speak anything.

[4] They are called **brethren beloved of God. Beloved** speaks of *having been and continuing to be loved by God* (ἠγαπημένοι). As part of giving thanks (v 2), Paul refers to their **election** (ἐκλογὴν). Many take this term as *choosing*. There is little foundation for this. The term denotes those who take part in responding to God's call and are clothed in Christ's righteousness (Mt 22:1-14 [14]). Verse five should be taken together with this phrase-*knowing your election, that is, that* (**for**) *our gospel came not in word only....*

[5] The **gospel** (εὐαγγέλιον) is the good news of salvation from sin by faith in Jesus Christ alone (Isa 40:9, 52:7; Lk 4:17-19). "The writer speaks of "our gospel" in the sense that it has been entrusted to them to proclaim it, but its author is God...." (Bruce). Its content may be seen in the 'nut-shell gospel': 1 Cor 15:1-4. The accomplishment of their election was affected by divine **power** (δυνάμει), the presence and working of **the Holy Spirit**, and *with* much assurance (πληροφορίᾳ πολλῇ). This ministry, inspired of the Spirit, has not passed with time. **As you know what manner of men we were** compares those who brought the message to the legitimacy of the message itself.

[6] Paul's co-workers so followed Christ in word and deed that they could be a "model of a Christ-like life for those who had no firsthand knowledge of Christ" (Findlay). The power of example cannot be misunderstood or overestimated. To be **followers** means to *imitate*. Our word mimic comes from it (*mimeomai*). The Thessalonians followed Paul *although* **having received the word in much affliction. With much joy** should go with the first part of the verse. **And you became followers of us, and of the Lord, with joy of the Spirit, although having received the word** *amid* **much affliction....**

[7] The result of their commitment: they become (**were**) an **example** worthy of imitation. The word **example** (τύπον, *type*) was used of molds or templates used to make clay pots. All of Greece, both Macedonia in the central/northern territory and Achaia, the southern area, were learning from their example.

[8] The news of what happened in Thessalonica spread quickly and far like a trumpet blast, **for from you, the word of the Lord** *has* **sounded out** (ἐξήχηται). Since the news had spread so, Paul and his companions **need not to speak anything**, i.e., they had nothing to add.

... 49 ...

GREEK TEXT

[9] αὐτοὶ γὰρ περὶ ἡμῶν ἀπαγγέλλουσιν ὁποίαν εἴσοδον ἔσχομεν πρὸς ὑμᾶς, καὶ πῶς ἐπεστρέψατε πρὸς τὸν θεὸν ἀπὸ τῶν εἰδώλων δουλεύειν θεῷ ζῶντι καὶ ἀληθινῷ, [10] καὶ ἀναμένειν τὸν υἱὸν αὐτοῦ ἐκ τῶν οὐρανῶν, ὃν ἤγειρεν ἐκ [τῶν] νεκρῶν, Ἰησοῦν τὸν ῥυόμενον ἡμᾶς ἐκ τῆς ὀργῆς τῆς ἐρχομένης. [2:1] Αὐτοὶ γὰρ οἴδατε, ἀδελφοί, τὴν εἴσοδον ἡμῶν τὴν πρὸς ὑμᾶς ὅτι οὐ κενὴ γέγονεν, [2] ἀλλὰ προπαθόντες καὶ ὑβρισθέντες καθὼς οἴδατε ἐν Φιλίπποις ἐπαρρησια-σάμεθα ἐν τῷ θεῷ ἡμῶν λαλῆσαι πρὸς ὑμᾶς τὸ εὐαγγέλιον τοῦ θεοῦ ἐν πολλῷ ἀγῶνι.

REFERENCES

[9]
(Jer 10:1-12) Hear the word which the LORD speaks unto you, O house of Israel: [2] Thus saith the LORD, Learn not the way of the heathen, and be not dismayed at the signs of heaven; for the heathen are dismayed at them. [3] For the customs of the people are vain: for one cutteth a tree out of the forest, the work of the hands of the workman, with the axe. [4] They deck it with silver and with gold; they fasten it with nails and with hammers, that it move not. [5] They are upright as the palm tree, but speak not: they must needs be borne, because they cannot go. Be not afraid of them; for they cannot do evil, neither also is it in them to do good. [6] Forasmuch as there is none like unto thee, O LORD; thou art great, and thy name is great in might. [7] Who would not fear thee, O King of nations? for to thee doth it appertain: forasmuch as among all the wise men of the nations, and in all their kingdoms, there is none like unto thee. [8] But they are altogether brutish and foolish: the stock is a doctrine of vanities. [9] Silver spread into plates is brought from Tarshish, and gold from Uphaz, the work of the workman, and of the hands of the founder: blue and purple is their clothing: they are all the work of cunning men. [10] But the LORD is the true God, he is the living God, and an everlasting king: at his wrath the earth shall tremble, and the nations shall not be able to abide his indignation. [11] Thus shall you say unto them, The gods that have not made the heavens and the earth, even they shall perish from the earth, and from under these heavens. [12] He hath made the earth by his power, he hath established the world by his wisdom, and hath stretched out the heavens by his discretion.
(Ac 14:15) And saying, Sirs, why do you these things? We also are men of like passions with you, and preach unto you that ye should turn from these vanities unto the living God, which made heaven, and earth, and the sea, and all things that are therein:
[2]
(Ac 16:16-40) Then came he to Derbe and Lystra: and, behold, a certain disciple was there, named Timothy, the son of a certain woman, which was a Jewess, and believed; but his father was a Greek: [2] Which was well reported of by the brethren that were at Lystra and Iconium. [3] Him would Paul have to go forth with him; and took and circumcised him because of the Jews which were in those quarters: for they knew all that his father was a Greek. [4] And as they went through the cities, they delivered them the decrees for to keep, that were ordained of the apostles and elders which were at Jerusalem.

1 THESSALONIANS 1:9-2:2

[1:9– 2:2]
[9] For they them-
selves show of us
what manner of
entering in we had
unto you, and how
you turned to God
from idols, to serve
the living and true
God,
[10] And to wait for
his Son from heaven,
whom he raised from
the dead, even Jesus,
who delivers us from
the wrath to come.
[2:1][π] For your-
selves, brethren,
know our entrance
in unto you, that it
was not in vain;
[2] But even after we
had suffered before,
and were shamefully
treated, as you know,
at Philippi, we were
bold in our God to
speak unto you the
gospel of God with
much contention.

[9] **Show** is in the sense of *report* (ἀπαγγέλλουσιν). Paul refers to **what manner of entering in** or *entrance* (εἴσοδον) the team had (2:1). The result of such an entrance was a turning to God from idols. "Early Christian evangelists did not attack idolatry, but rather presented Jesus. Conversion was not a turning from idols to God, but a turning to God from idols" (Richards). Bruce states, "There is only one God, who, by contrast with idols, can be described as 'a living (and true) God'" (Jer 10:1-12; Ac 14:15).

[10] **You turned to God,** *from* **idols,** *to* **serve... and** *to* **wait for his Son.** Believers have a living expectation and motivation: the coming of **God's Son from heaven.** The **wrath to come** is literal and definite, *the coming wrath* (τῆς ὀργῆς τῆς ἐρχομένης). It refers to a definite event- the tribulation period. With believers *rescued* (ῥυόμενον) at the rapture, God will pour out his righteous fury on unbelief and rebellion.

Verse one begins the body of the letter. This first and longest section is called a narratio: a recounting of events. This section seeks to assess the events that have occurred, to solidify Paul's relationship with the Thessalonians, and to distinguish their conduct from false teachers. It must be remembered that Paul's stay in Thessalonica was very brief and this section is a reflection and treatment of that situation.

[1][π] The phrase **in vain** (οὐ κενὴ) is in the sense of *not without effect* (NAB) or not lacking in purpose or effect. Verse two and following certainly contrast the idea that their entrance was in vain.

[2] Circumstances did not stop the apostles' work. *Although having* **suffered before** and *although* **shamefully treated,** they **were bold to speak the gospel of God.** The difficulties at **Philippi** are found in Ac 16:16-40. To be **shamefully treated** (ὑβρισθέντες) may indicate *insolently treated* (NAB) or to suffer criminal violence (Findlay). Their boldness is drawn from the divine source: **in our God. With much contention** (ἀγῶνι, our word agony is derived from this word) may be translated *amid great conflict* (Bruce).

Christians are not told to prepare for the coming wrath. They will be rescued from it.

GREEK TEXT

[3] ἡ γὰρ παράκλησις ἡμῶν οὐκ ἐκ πλάνης οὐδὲ ἐξ ἀκαθαρσίας οὐδὲ ἐν δόλῳ, [4] ἀλλὰ καθὼς δεδοκιμάσμεθα ὑπὸ τοῦ θεοῦ πιστευθῆναι τὸ εὐαγγέλιον οὕτως λαλοῦμεν, οὐχ ὡς ἀνθρώποις ἀρέσκοντες ἀλλὰ θεῷ τῷ δοκιμάζοντι τὰς καρδίας ἡμῶν. [5] οὔτε γάρ ποτε ἐν λόγῳ κολακείας ἐγενήθημεν, καθὼς οἴδατε, οὔτε ἐν προφάσει πλεονεξίας, θεὸς μάρτυς, [6] οὔτε ζητοῦντες ἐξ ἀνθρώπων δόξαν, οὔτε ἀφ' ὑμῶν οὔτε ἀπ' ἄλλων, [7] δυνάμενοι ἐν βάρει εἶναι ὡς Χριστοῦ ἀπόστολοι, ἀλλὰ ἐγενήθημεν νήπιοι ἐν μέσῳ ὑμῶν. ὡς ἐὰν τροφὸς θάλπῃ τὰ ἑαυτῆς τέκνα,

REFERENCES

[3]
(1 Cor 14:3) But he that prophesies speaks unto men to edification, and exhortation, and comfort.
(1 Tim 4:13) Till I come, give attendance to reading, to exhortation, to doctrine.
(Ac 13:15) And after the reading of the law and the prophets the rulers of the synagogue sent unto them, saying, Ye men and brethren, if you have any word of exhortation for the people, say on.
(2 Pet 2:1-3) But there were false prophets also among the people, even as there shall be false teachers among you, who privily shall bring in damnable heresies, even denying the Lord that bought them, and bring upon themselves swift destruction. [2] And many shall follow their pernicious ways; by reason of whom the way of truth shall be evil spoken of. [3] And through covetousness shall they with feigned words make merchandise of you: whose judgment now of a long time lingers not, and their damnation slumbers not.
[4]
(Ro 8:27) And he that searches the hearts knows what is the mind of the Spirit, because he makes intercession for the saints according to the will of God.
(Ac 1:24) And they prayed, and said, Thou, Lord, which knows the hearts of all men....
(Rev 2:23) And I will kill her children with death; and all the churches shall know that I am he which searches the reins and hearts: and I will give unto every one of you according to your works.
[5]
(Ac 27:30) But as the sailors were trying to escape from the ship and had let down the ship's boat into the sea, on the pretense of intending to lay out anchors from the bow (NASB)
(Jn 15:22) If I had not come and spoken unto them, they had not had sin: but now they have no cloak for their sin.
(Phil 1:18) What then? notwithstanding, every way, whether in pretence, or in truth, Christ is preached; and I therein do rejoice, yea, and will rejoice.
(2 Cor 2:17) For we are not as many, which corrupt the word of God: but as of sincerity, but as of God, in the sight of God speak we in Christ.
(Ex 20:17) Thou shalt not covet thy neighbor's house, thou shalt not covet thy neighbor's wife, nor his manservant, nor his maidservant, nor his ox, nor his ass, nor any thing that is thy neighbor's.

[2:3-7]
[3] For our exhort-
tation was not of
deceit, nor of un-
cleanness, nor in
guile;
[4] But as we were
allowed of God to be
put in trust with the
gospel, even so we
speak; not as
pleasing men but
God, who trieth our
hearts.
[5] For neither at any
time used we
flattering words, as
you know, nor a
cloak of covetous-
ness, God is witness;
[6] Nor of men
sought we glory,
neither of you, nor
yet of others, when
we might have been
burdensome, as the
apostles of Christ.
[7] But we were
gentle among you,
even as a nurse
cherisheth her
children.

[3] Paul now disclaims certain activities that were well known both in his day and in ours. Their **exhortation** or *urging* (παράκλησις)(I Cor 14:3; I Tim 4:13; Ac 13:15) **was not of**... Findlay notes, "For our appeal (is) not of (does not proceed from) error [**deceit**], nor from impurity [**uncleanness**], nor (is it made) in **guile**." **Deceit** (ἐκ πλάνης) is the use of error. **Uncleanness** (ἀκαθαρσίας) denotes impure character, and **in guile** (δόλῳ) suggests with cunning (2 Pt 2:1-3).

[4] Paul and his team (**we**) **were** *approved* or *judged worthy* (δεδοκιμάσμεθα, **allowed**) to be *entrusted* (πιστευθῆναι) **with the gospel.** As part of this trust, the motive and methods of **pleasing men** was absent. Ministry does not succeed based on opinion polls. The words **allowed** and **trieth** are from the same verb (δεδοκιμάσμεθα). God *has approved and continues to approve* their **hearts.** This is a bold assertion. It is not just their methods, minds, and training, but the integrity of their hearts that has been determined (Ro 8:27; Ac 1:24; Rev 2:23).

Words are the tools of deception.

[5] **Flattering words** or more literally *in the word of flattery* (κολακείας). Findlay says that flattery is a "sinister self-interested compliment". In this context, flattery is "a flattery calculated to deceive" (Frame). Paul regarded this vice as "conduct extremely repugnant" (Robertson). What is a **cloak** (προφάσει) in this context? It is a *pretext* or something pretended for gain (Ac 27:30; Jn 15:22; Phil 1:18; 2 Cor 2:17, *For we are not as the many, adulterating the word of God, but as of sincerity -- but as of God; in the presence of God, in Christ we do speak.* [Young's]). Wanamaker calls it a "means of hiding one's real motives" and "the deception with which greed regularly operates" (Wanamaker). **Thou shalt not covet....** (Ex 20:17). The word **covetousness** comes from two Greek words. The first word meaning *more* (πλεον), is fused to the second word meaning *to have* (εξίας). Thus, it means to pursue having more. In Mark 7:22, it is included along with fornication, adultery, murder and pride. The mission team did not come under false pretences for the sake of gain. **God** is summoned as a **witness** (μάρτυς) in behalf of Paul's team.

[6] Reputation and fame are also polluted motives for ministry. Service for Christ does not require a spot light. The second half of verse six goes with verse seven.

GREEK TEXT

[7] δυνάμενοι ἐν βάρει εἶναι ὡς Χριστοῦ ἀπόστολοι, ἀλλὰ ἐγενήθημεν νήπιοι ἐν μέσῳ ὑμῶν. ὡς ἐὰν τροφὸς θάλπῃ τὰ ἑαυτῆς τέκνα, [8] οὕτως ὁμειρόμενοι ὑμῶν εὐδοκοῦμεν μεταδοῦναι ὑμῖν οὐ μόνον τὸ εὐαγγέλιον τοῦ θεοῦ ἀλλὰ καὶ τὰς ἑαυτῶν ψυχάς, διότι ἀγαπητοὶ ἡμῖν ἐγενήθητε. [9] μνημονεύετε γάρ, ἀδελφοί, τὸν κόπον ἡμῶν καὶ τὸν μόχθοννυκτὸς καὶ ἡμέρας ἐργαζόμενοι πρὸς τὸ μὴ ἐπιβαρῆσαί τινα ὑμῶν ἐκηρύξαμεν εἰς ὑμᾶς τὸ εὐαγγέλιον τοῦ θεοῦ. [10] ὑμεῖς μάρτυρες καὶ ὁ θεός, ὡς ὁσίως καὶ δικαίως καὶ ἀμέμπτως ὑμῖν τοῖς πιστεύουσιν ἐγενήθημεν, [11] καθάπερ οἴδατε ὡς ἕνα ἕκαστον ὑμῶν ὡς πατὴρ τέκνα ἑαυτοῦ

REFERENCES

[7]
(2 Tim 2:24) And the servant of the Lord must not strive; but be gentle unto all men, apt to teach, patient,
(1 Tim 3:3) Not given to wine, no striker, not greedy of filthy lucre; but patient, not a brawler, not covetous;
(Titus 1:7) For a bishop must be blameless, as the steward of God; not self willed, not soon angry, not given to wine, no striker, not given to filthy lucre;
[9]
(I Cor 9:12-18) If others be partakers of this power over you, are not we rather? Nevertheless we have not used this power; but suffer all things, lest we should hinder the gospel of Christ. [13] Do ye not know that they which minister about holy things live of the things of the temple? and they which wait at the altar are partakers with the altar? [14] Even so hath the Lord ordained that they which preach the gospel should live of the gospel. [15] But I have used none of these things: neither have I written these things, that it should be so done unto me: for it were better for me to die, than that any man should make my glorying void. [16] For though I preach the gospel, I have nothing to glory of: for necessity is laid upon me; yea, woe is unto me, if I preach not the gospel! [17]   For if I do this thing willingly, I have a reward: but if against my will, a dispensation of the gospel is committed unto me. [18] What is my reward then? Verily that, when I preach the gospel, I may make the gospel of Christ without charge, that I abuse not my power in the gospel.

TYPICAL BODY ELEMENTS

o———————o

TOPIC (S)
-disclosure formula
-challenge to action
-request/injunction
-expressions of joy
-expressions of astonishment
-autobiographical information
-travelogue
-issues and answers

PARENESIS:
-moral injunctions
-virtue/vice list
-haustafeln (house codes)

[2:7-11]

[7] But we were gentle among you, even as a nurse cherisheth her children.
[8] So, being affectionately desirous of you, we were willing to have imparted unto you not the gospel of God only, but also our own souls, because you were dear unto us.
[9] For you remember, brethren, our labor and travail; for laboring night and day, because we would not be chargeable unto any of you, we preached unto you the gospel of God.
[10] You are witnesses, and God also, how holily and justly and unblamably we behaved ourselves among you that believe,
[11] As you know how we exhorted and encouraged and charged every one of you, as a father doth his children,

Although being able in weight to be as apostles of Christ, on the contrary, we were gentle among you.... The privileges and place, fully just to the apostles, was declined, supporting their efforts to be **gentle** and loving to their followers. Two similes (ὡς, **as**) are used to describe their disposition to the Thessalonians (v 11). Their **gentleness** (ἤπιον, 2 Tm 2:24) was as a mother-nurse *cares for* **her children**. Character that is agreeable is mandatory for those in the work of the pastorate (1 Tim 3:3; Titus 1:7).

[8] Consequently (**so**), they were **affectionately desirous** (ὁμειρόμενοι) or had great affection for the people, such that their **own souls** were offered. This text teaches that there is no gospel ministry without the expenditure of self. *Beloved* and **dear** are the same root word (1:4).

Many wandering charlatans made their
way about the Greek world,
peddling their religious
or philosophical nostrums, and living
at the expense of their devotees. Bruce

[9] In support of verse eight (**for**), we find the evidence that their souls were a part of the gospel ministry in Thessalonica. They (**we**) worked to **not** *overburden* **any**. Thus, they relinquished their monetary privileges (I Cor 9:12-18). The **gospel** is referenced five times in the narratio section.

[10] **Witnesses** are called to validate the conduct of the missionaries. They are those who are qualified to testify: the Thessalonians **and God**. Frame notes, "A man is [ὁσίως, **holy**] who is in general devoted to God's service; a man is [δικαίως, **just**] who comes up to a specific standard of righteousness; and a man is [ἀμέμπτως, **blameless**] who in the light of a given norm is without reproach."

[11] Hoffman notes, "To **exhort** is speech that addresses itself to the will, to **encourage** [*console, cheer?*, 5:14] to the sensibilities, while to **charge** [*affirm*] signalizes the impressive seriousness with which the speaker personally vouches for what he says." These actions were performed individually-**every** or *each* **one of you. As** begins the second simile comparing their care and guidance with that of **a father** with **his children**. They were given maternal and paternal care.

GREEK TEXT

[12] παρακαλοῦντες ὑμᾶς καὶ παραμυθούμενοι καὶ μαρτυρόμενοι εἰς τὸ περιπατεῖν ὑμᾶς ἀξίως τοῦ θεοῦ τοῦ καλοῦντος ὑμᾶς εἰς τὴν ἑαυτοῦ βασιλείαν καὶ δόξαν. [13] Καὶ διὰ τοῦτο καὶ ἡμεῖς εὐχαριστοῦμεν τῷ θεῷ ἀδιαλείπτως, ὅτι παραλαβόντες λόγον ἀκοῆς παρ' ἡμῶν τοῦ θεοῦ ἐδέξασθε οὐ λόγον ἀνθρώπων ἀλλὰ καθώς ἐστιν ἀληθῶς λόγον θεοῦ, ὃς καὶ ἐνεργεῖται ἐν ὑμῖν τοῖς πιστεύουσιν. [14] ὑμεῖς γὰρ μιμηταὶ ἐγενήθητε, ἀδελφοί, τῶν ἐκκλησιῶν τοῦ θεοῦ τῶν οὐσῶν ἐν τῇ Ἰουδαίᾳ ἐν Χριστῷ Ἰησοῦ, ὅτι τὰ αὐτὰ ἐπάθετε καὶ ὑμεῖς ὑπὸ τῶν ἰδίων συμφυλετῶν καθὼς καὶ αὐτοὶ ὑπὸ τῶν Ἰουδαίων, [15] τῶν καὶ τὸν κύριον ἀποκτεινάντων Ἰησοῦν καὶ τοὺς προφήτας, καὶ ἡμᾶς ἐκδιωξάντων, καὶ θεῷ μὴ ἀρεσκόντων, καὶ πᾶσιν ἀνθρώποις ἐναντίων, [16] κωλυόντων ἡμᾶς τοῖς ἔθνεσιν λαλῆσαι ἵνα σωθῶσιν, εἰς τὸ ἀναπληρῶσαι αὐτῶν τὰς ἁμαρτίας πάντοτε. ἔφθασεν δὲ ἐπ' αὐτοὺς ἡ ὀργὴ εἰς τέλος. [17][π] Ἡμεῖς δέ, ἀδελφοί, ἀπορφανισθέντες ἀφ' ὑμῶν πρὸς καιρὸν ὥρας, προσώπῳ οὐ καρδίᾳ, περισσοτέρως ἐσπουδάσαμεν τὸ πρόσωπον ὑμῶν ἰδεῖν ἐν πολλῇ ἐπιθυμίᾳ. [18] διότι ἠθελήσαμεν ἐλθεῖν πρὸς ὑμᾶς, ἐγὼ μὲν Παῦλος καὶ ἅπαξ καὶ δίς, καὶ ἐνέκοψεν ἡμᾶς ὁ Σατανᾶς.

REFERENCES

[12]
(Phil 1:27) Only let your conversation be as it becomes the gospel of Christ: that whether I come and see you, or else be absent, I may hear of your affairs, that you stand fast in one spirit, with one mind striving together for the faith of the gospel;
(Eph 4:1) I therefore, the prisoner of the Lord, beseech you that you walk worthy of the vocation wherewith you are called,
(1 Cor 15:23-24) But every man in his own order: Christ the first fruits; afterward they that are Christ's at his coming. [24] Then cometh the end, when he shall have delivered up the kingdom to God, even the Father; when he shall have put down all rule and all authority and power.
[13]
(Ga 1:11-12) But I certify you, brethren, that the gospel which was preached of me is not after man. [12] For I neither received it of man, neither was I taught it, but by the revelation of Jesus Christ.
[14]
(Eph 3:14-15) For this cause I bow my knees unto the Father of our Lord Jesus Christ, [15] Of whom the whole family in heaven and earth is named,
[16]
(Ac 17:13) But when the Jews of Thessalonica had knowledge that the word of God was preached of Paul at Berea, they came thither also, and stirred up the people.
[17]
(Ac 17:10, 14) And the brethren immediately sent away Paul and Silas by night unto Berea: who coming thither went into the synagogue of the Jews. [14] And then immediately the brethren sent away Paul to go as it were to the sea: but Silas and Timothy abode there still.
(Phil 1:27) Only let your conversation be as it becomes the gospel of Christ: that whether I come and see you, or else be absent, I may hear of your affairs, that you stand fast in one spirit, with one mind striving together for the faith of the gospel;
[18]
(Ro 15:22) For which cause also I have been much hindered from coming to you.

[2:12-18]
[12] That you would walk worthy of God, who hath called you unto his kingdom and glory.
[13] For this cause also thank we God without ceasing because, when you received the word of God which you heard from us, you received it not as the word of men, but as it is in truth, the word of God, which effectually worketh also in you that believe.
[14] For you, brethren, became followers of the churches of God which in Judea are in Christ Jesus; for you also have suffered like things of your own countrymen, even as they have of the Jews,
[15] Who both killed the Lord Jesus and their own prophets, and have persecuted us; and they please not God, and are contrary to all men,
[16] Forbidding us to speak to the Gentiles that they might be saved, to fill up their sins always; for the wrath is come upon them to the uttermost.
[17][π] But we, brethren, being taken from you for a short time in presence, not in heart, endeavored the more abundantly to see your face with great desire.
[18] Wherefore, we would have come unto you, even I, Paul, once and again; but Satan hindered us.

[12] The entire purpose (**that you would**) of their urgings was a **walk worthy of God** (Phil 1:27; Eph 4:1). It is God who *summons* (καλοῦντος) us to **his kingdom and glory** (1 Cor 15:23-28).

[13] Paul now resumes thanksgiving for them, noting that they **received** or *took* the **word** as it is **the word of God** (Ga 1:11-12). Teaching and doctrine either fall toward **the word of men** or **the word of God**. **The word of God** *effectively* or *thoroughly works* (ἐνεργεῖται) in those who **believe**. I have **no greater joy than to hear that my children walk in truth** (3 John 4). Truth exists and must be obeyed.

[14] The Thessalonians have joined the family of God (Eph 3:14-15) and now share similar trouble with the **churches in Judea**. The **godly shall suffer persecution** (2 Tm 3:12).

[15] Paul has no reservations citing the transgressions *of his own people*. It is with care and propriety that he speaks of the failings of the Cretans in Titus, citing Epimenides- who was a Cretan. Regarding the Jews, he was the authority.

No legitimate religion
practices
hatred and murder.

[16] **The Jews** are *hindering* or *obstructing* (κωλυόντων) presently, the evangelism of the Gentiles (Ac 17:13), *but wrath has begun to come upon them pointing to their end*.

[17] [π] A new paragraph begins: **but** or *now* (δέ), **we**.... Paul indicates their situation as **being taken from** them (Ac 17:10, 14). This verb is more literally *having been orphaned* (Gk., *orphanizo*) **from you.** "It describes here the severing of new-found and tenderly attached 'brothers'" (Bruce). Although not present, Paul certainly did not lack in deep seated affection for his new converts (**in heart**)(Phil 1:27).

[18] The phrase **once and again** is an idiom for *more than once*. The difficulty: the *Adversary* (**Satan**). He **hindered** or obstructed the way to the Thessalonians (Ro 15:22). Findlay notes that the hindering did not obstruct the willing but the endeavoring. This word (ἐνέκοψεν) is used elsewhere of cutting off a road, which is appropriate in the context. Note Gal 5:7, **You were running well; who hindered you from obeying the truth?** Satan and his devotees work feverishly to detour the work of the gospel.

GREEK TEXT

[19] τίς γὰρ ἡμῶν ἐλπὶς ἢ χαρὰ ἢ στέφανος καυχήσεως— ἢ οὐχὶ καὶ ὑμεῖς ἔμπροσθεν τοῦ κυρίου ἡμῶν Ἰησοῦ ἐν τῇ αὐτοῦ παρουσίᾳ; [20] ὑμεῖς γάρ ἐστε ἡ δόξα ἡμῶν καὶ ἡ χαρά.

[1][π] Διὸ μηκέτι στέγοντες εὐδοκήσαμεν καταλειφθῆναι ἐν Ἀθήναις μόνοι, [2] καὶ ἐπέμψαμεν Τιμόθεον, τὸν ἀδελφὸν ἡμῶν καὶ Ιδιάκονον Ι [UBS, συνεργὸν] τοῦ θεοῦ ἐν τῷ εὐαγγελίῳ τοῦ Χριστοῦ, εἰς τὸ στηρίξαι ὑμᾶς καὶ παρακαλέσαι ὑπὲρ τῆς πίστεως ὑμῶν [3] τὸ μηδένα σαίνεσθαι ἐν ταῖς θλίψεσιν ταύταις. αὐτοὶ γὰρ οἴδατε ὅτι εἰς τοῦτο κείμεθα· [4] καὶ γὰρ ὅτε πρὸς ὑμᾶς ἦμεν, προελέγομεν ὑμῖν ὅτι μέλλομεν θλίβεσθαι, καθὼς καὶ ἐγένετο καὶ οἴδατε.

REFERENCES

[1]
(Ac 17:15) And they that conducted Paul brought him unto Athens: and receiving a commandment unto Silas and Timothy for to come to him with all speed, they departed.
[2]
(Ac 14:21-22) And when they had preached the gospel to that city, and had taught many, they returned again to Lystra, and to Iconium, and Antioch, [22] Confirming the souls of the disciples, and exhorting them to continue in the faith, and that we must through much tribulation enter into the kingdom of God.
(Ro 1:11) For I long to see you, that I may impart unto you some spiritual gift, to the end ye may be established;
[3]
(1 Pet 4:1) Forasmuch then as Christ hath suffered for us in the flesh, arm yourselves likewise with the same mind: for he that hath suffered in the flesh hath ceased from sin
(Ac 14:21-22) And when they had preached the gospel to that city, and had taught many, they returned again to Lystra, and to Iconium, and Antioch, [22] Confirming the souls of the disciples, and exhorting them to continue in the faith, and that we must through much tribulation enter into the kingdom of God.
[4]
(2 Cor 7:5) For, when we were come into Macedonia, our flesh had no rest, but we were troubled on every side; without were fightings, within were fears.

APOSTLE PAUL
V.
THE JEWS
Docket Number: BI -NT-1 THES -2-14-FF

(1) 15 §§ Murder: the Lord Jesus Christ.
(2) 15 §§ Murder: the prophets.
(3) 15 §§ Persecution.
(4) 15 §§ Contrary to humankind.
(5) 16 §§ Hindering Gospel ministry.

[2:19– 3:4]

[19] For what is our hope, or joy, or crown of rejoicing? Are not even you in the presence of our Lord Jesus Christ at his coming?
[20] For you are our glory and joy.
[1][π] Wherefore, when we could no longer forbear, we thought it good to be left at Athens alone,
[2] And sent Timothy, our brother and minister of God, and our fellow worker in the gospel of Christ, to establish you, and to comfort you concerning your faith,
[3] That no man should be moved by these afflictions; for you yourselves know that we are appointed to these things.
[4] For verily, when we were with you, we told you before that we should suffer tribulation, even as it came to pass, and you know.

[19] The two questions in this verse are answered in verse twenty. To see those who turned to **Christ** *before* (**in the presence of,** ἔμπροσθεν) the **Lord at his coming,** i.e., the rapture, will be the great prize for Paul, like the *victor's wreath* (στέφανος, **crown**) was to a competitor. This is the first of six references in the Thessalonian correspondence to a **coming** (παρουσία, *parousia*). See p 99.

[20] The team glories in and receives **joy** from the converts in Thessalonica. They cheer them.

[3:1][π] **Wherefore** (Διὸ) points back to previous information and tells of how that information has directed them. In other words, because of their love and inability to come personally (vv 17-20), Paul now chooses another avenue of contact: **Timothy.** Paul visits **Athens** beginning in Acts 17:15.

[2] Timothy's mission is summarized by three infinitives: **to establish, to comfort,** and to prevent them from **being moved** (v 3). All three of these actions function toward the strengthening of their **faith.** It was a standing work of ministry to strengthen or make converts resolute (στηρίξαι, **establish**) in the faith (Ac 14:21-22; Ro 1:11). Not surprisingly, this word is used four of six times in Paul's letters to the newly converted Thessalonians (I Thes 3:2, 13; 2 Thes 2:17, 3:3). They also need **comfort** (παρακαλέσαι) in the difficulties engendered by their new found faith.

[3] The third function for Timothy is stated negatively and precisely: **that no man be moved....** This clause gives the purpose of Timothy's mission beginning in verse two. The term **moved** (σαίνεσθαι) is very rare in Greek writings. Most take it as *swayed, agitated,* or *unsettled. Afflictions* (θλίψεσιν) are a part of the Christian walk to the point that we *remain* (κείμεθα, **are appointed**) unto them (1 Pt 4:1; Ac 14:21-22). His task was to strengthen, console, and stabilize. "In the difficult situation the Thessalonians had faced without their spiritual mentors, they might have renounced their Christian beliefs and way of life" (Wanamaker). But they did not.

[4] **Verily** or *for even* **when we were with you....** (not the "verily" of the gospels). The word **should** has evolved to suggest what is best to happen. Here it simply means **we** *were about to be afflicted* (θλίβεσθαι, 2 Co 7:5).

Dwight Pentecost notes seventeen distinctions between the rapture or translation and the second advent.
Things to Come, p 206

GREEK TEXT

[5] διὰ τοῦτο κἀγὼ μηκέτι στέγων ἔπεμψα εἰς τὸ γνῶναι τὴν πίστιν ὑμῶν, μή πως ἐπείρασεν ὑμᾶς ὁ πειράζων καὶ εἰς κενὸν γένηται ὁ κόπος ἡμῶν. [6] Ἄρτι δὲ ἐλθόντος Τιμοθέου πρὸς ἡμᾶς ἀφ' ὑμῶν καὶ εὐαγγελισαμένου ἡμῖν τὴν πίστιν καὶ τὴν ἀγάπην ὑμῶν, καὶ ὅτι ἔχετε μνείαν ἡμῶν ἀγαθὴν πάντοτε, ἐπιποθοῦντες ἡμᾶς ἰδεῖν καθάπερ καὶ ἡμεῖς ὑμᾶς, [7] διὰ τοῦτο παρεκλήθημεν, ἀδελφοί, ἐφ' ὑμῖν ἐπὶ πάσῃ τῇ ἀνάγκῃ καὶ θλίψει ἡμῶν διὰ τῆς ὑμῶν πίστεως, [8] ὅτι νῦν ζῶμεν ἐὰν ὑμεῖς στήκετε ἐν κυρίῳ. [9] τίνα γὰρ εὐχαριστίαν δυνάμεθα τῷ θεῷ ἀνταποδοῦναι περὶ ὑμῶν ἐπὶ πάσῃ τῇ χαρᾷ ᾗ χαίρομεν δι' ὑμᾶς ἔμπροσθεν τοῦ θεοῦ ἡμῶν, [10] νυκτὸς καὶ ἡμέρας ὑπερεκπερισσοῦ δεόμενοι εἰς τὸ ἰδεῖν ὑμῶν τὸ πρόσωπον καὶ καταρτίσαι τὰ ὑστερήματα τῆς πίστεως ὑμῶν;
[11][π] Αὐτὸς δὲ ὁ θεὸς καὶ πατὴρ ἡμῶν καὶ ὁ κύριος ἡμῶν Ἰησοῦς κατευθύναι τὴν ὁδὸν ἡμῶν πρὸς ὑμᾶς· [12] ὑμᾶς δὲ ὁ κύριος πλεονάσαι καὶ περισσεύσαι τῇ ἀγάπῃ εἰς ἀλλήλους καὶ εἰς πάντας, καθάπερ καὶ ἡμεῖς εἰς ὑμᾶς, [13] εἰς τὸ στηρίξαι ὑμῶν τὰς καρδίας ἀμέμπτους ἐν ἁγιωσύνῃ ἔμπροσθεν τοῦ θεοῦ καὶ πατρὸς ἡμῶν ἐν τῇ παρουσίᾳ τοῦ κυρίου ἡμῶν Ἰησοῦ μετὰ πάντων τῶν ἁγίων αὐτοῦ |omit| [UBS, ἀμήν].

REFERENCES

[5]
(2 Cor 11:28) Beside those things that are without, that which cometh upon me daily, the care of all the churches.
[8]
(I Cor 16:13) Be on the alert, stand firm in the faith, act like men, be strong (NASB).
(Gal 5:1) Stand fast therefore in the liberty wherewith Christ hath made us free, and be not entangled again with the yoke of bondage.
(Phil 4:1) Therefore, my brethren dearly beloved and longed for, my joy and crown, so stand fast in the Lord, my dearly beloved.
(2 Thes 2:15) Therefore, brethren, stand fast, and hold the traditions which you have been taught, whether by word, or our epistle.
(Ro 14:4) Who art thou that judges another man's servant? to his own master he stands or falls. Yea, he shall be held up: for God is able to make him stand.
[9-10]
(Heb 13:20-21) Now the God of peace, that brought again from the dead our Lord Jesus, that great shepherd of the sheep, through the blood of the everlasting covenant, [21] Make you perfect in every good work to do his will, working in you that which is well-pleasing in his sight, through Jesus Christ; to whom be glory for ever and ever. Amen.
[11]
(Jn 13:35) By this shall all men know that you are my disciples, if you have love one to another.

[3:5-13]

[5] For this cause, when I could no longer forbear, I sent to know your faith, lest by some means the tempter have tempted you, and our labor be in vain.
[6] But now, when Timothy came from you unto us, and brought us good tidings of your faith and love, and that you have good remembrance of us always, desiring greatly to see us, as we also to see you;
[7] Therefore, brethren, we were comforted over you in all our affliction and distress by your faith;
[8] For now we live, if you stand fast in the Lord.
[9] For what thanks can we render to God again for you, for all the joy with which we joy for your sakes before our God,
[10] Night and day praying exceedingly that we might see your face, and might perfect that which is lacking in your faith?
[11][π] Now God himself and our Father, and our Lord Jesus Christ, direct our way unto you.
[12] And the Lord make you to increase and abound in love one toward another, and toward all men, even as we do toward you,
[13] To the end he may establish your hearts unblamable in holiness before God, even our Father at the coming of our Lord Jesus Christ with all his saints.

[5] The same term **forbear** or *endure* (στέγων) appears as in 4:1. Bornemann notes "τὴν πίστιν [the **faith**] forms the all comprising and fundamental concept for the whole life of Christianity as it is called into existence by the Gospel". The state of their personal **faith** was the heaviness of Paul's heart (2 Cor 11:28). His apprehension or concern was that *the one who tempts* (The Devil, the adversary of the brethren), *tempted you*, resulting in fruitless **labor**.
[6] The term **good tidings** (εὐαγγελισαμένου) usually is technical, denoting the preaching of the gospel. Here it is generic: *good news*. The report that we know of is of a vibrant **faith and love** and an intact relationship with the team. The **now when**, suggests that this letter was written immediately after Timothy's return and report to Paul.
[7] The news administered **comfort** although they (the team) were *amid* **affliction and distress**.
[8] This is one of many great ministerial verses of the Bible. Bruce notes, "The news of your unwavering faith and love is the very breath of life to us." To **stand fast** or *make a stand* (στήκετε) is a command directed to other churches (I Cor 16:13; Ga 5:1; Phil 4:1; 2 Thes 2:15; Ro 14:4).
[9-10] They have **joy** that allows them to *rejoice* (joy). With such a report, what need was there for perfecting? What lacked? Findlay says "the **lacking** things point to what was lacking not *in* but *to* the faith" (Heb 13:20-21). Their conversion was recent and their progress remarkable, but it still needed perfecting and maturity.

Verses eleven through thirteen are a prayer-wish (the first of five in the Thessalonian letters). These are open appeals to God in behalf of those who are reading them.

[11-12][π] **Now** (δὲ) *may* **God himself ...direct our way** ...*may* **the Lord make you to increase and abound**.... Paul openly requests divine help to overcome the obstacles in visiting the Thessalonians. **Love** has been exemplified and needs to continue among the brethren and others (Jn 13:35).
[13] What is the **end** or purpose of his desires– that their **hearts** be blameless (ἀμέμπτους) in sanctification (**holiness**) at the **coming** (παρουσία, *parousia*) of our Lord with **all his saints**.

GREEK TEXT

[1][π] Λοιπὸν lomitl [UBS, οὖν], ἀδελφοί, ἐρωτῶμεν ὑμᾶς καὶ παρακαλοῦμεν ἐν κυρίῳ Ἰησοῦ, ἵνα καθὼς παρελάβετε παρ' ἡμῶν τὸ πῶς δεῖ ὑμᾶς περιπατεῖν καὶ ἀρέσκειν θεῷ, καθὼς καὶ περιπατεῖτε, ἵνα περισσεύητε μᾶλλον. [2] οἴδατε γὰρ τίνας παραγγελίας ἐδώκαμεν ὑμῖν διὰ τοῦ κυρίου Ἰησοῦ. [3] τοῦτο γάρ ἐστιν θέλημα τοῦ θεοῦ, ὁ ἁγιασμὸς ὑμῶν, ἀπέχεσθαι ὑμᾶς ἀπὸ τῆς πορνείας,

REFERENCES

[3]
(1 Cor 7:8-9) I say therefore to the unmarried and widows, it is good for them if they abide even as I. [9] But if they cannot contain, let them marry: for it is better to marry than to burn.

TOPIC # 1: ABSTINENCE

Verse one begins a distinct section within the body of the letter. The author now introduces five topics in an arrangement that might be called issues and answers. Some have labeled this section a probatio, since it expounds and proves the matters at hand. Each issue begins with typical formulaic markers (See chart).

[4:1-3]

[1][π] Furthermore, then, we beseech you, brethren, and exhort you by the Lord Jesus, that as you have received of us how you ought to walk and to please God, so you would abound more and more.

[2] For you know what commandments we gave you by the Lord Jesus.

[3] For this is the will of God, even your sanctification, that you should abstain from fornication;

[1][π] Verses one and two may serve as an introduction to the topic. *Finally therefore*, (Λοιπὸν |*omit* |[UBS, οὖν]) *we are requesting* (beseech) and *exhorting* by the Lord Jesus. This last phrase indicates that the appeal is not merely personal. They had received *how it is mandatory* or *obligatory* (δεῖ, ought) to walk- indicating life style choices, and to please God, indicating the purpose and consequence of that walk. The urging is not to start, but to press on and not be hindered (abound more and more).

[2] A reminder is appropriate to begin expounding the topic (For you know). It is itself a commentary on the human spirit that Paul consistently needs to remind and reinforce what he has already taught in person. The agent (the Lord Jesus) through (by) whom their commandments (*directives*) came is the Lord. Paul's team was the conduit of the truth.

[3] The grammar of this verse is challenging. This is the will of God: even your sanctification- *for* you to abstain.... The will of God (θέλημα τοῦ θεοῦ), as stated in this verse, is something concrete, fixed, not discerned, non negotiable. It refers to what God wants, i.e., demands. One who is consecrated is considered sanctified (ἁγιασμὸς) or *holy*. Frame aptly says that "true consecration being moral as well as religious demands sexual purity." Marriage is honorable... and the bed undefiled (He 13:4)(1 Cor 7:8-9).

	Introductory Element	Brethren?	Disposition
4:1	Finally, therefore...	Brethren	We Ask / Exhort
4:9	Now (δὲ) concerning...	...	You need not that I write
4:10b	Now (δὲ) ...	Brethren	We Exhort
4:13	Now (δὲ) concerning...	Brethren	I don't want you to be ignorant
5:1	Now (δὲ) concerning...	Brethren	You have no need that I write

GREEK TEXT

[3] τοῦτο γὰρ ἐστιν θέλημα τοῦ θεοῦ, ὁ ἁγιασμὸς ὑμῶν, ἀπέχεσθαι ὑμᾶς ἀπὸ τῆς πορνείας, [4] εἰδέναι ἕκαστον ὑμῶν τὸ ἑαυτοῦ σκεῦος κτᾶσθαι ἐν ἁγιασμῷ καὶ τιμῇ, [5] μὴ ἐν πάθει ἐπιθυμίας καθάπερ καὶ τὰ ἔθνη τὰ μὴ εἰδότα τὸν θεόν, [6] τὸ μὴ ὑπερβαίνειν καὶ πλεονεκτεῖν ἐν τῷ πράγματι τὸν ἀδελφὸν αὐτοῦ, διότι ἔκδικος κύριος περὶ πάντων τούτων, καθὼς καὶ προείπαμεν ὑμῖν καὶ διεμαρτυράμεθα. [7] οὐ γὰρ ἐκάλεσεν ἡμᾶς ὁ θεὸς ἐπὶ ἀκαθαρσίᾳ ἀλλ' ἐν ἁγιασμῷ.

REFERENCES

[3]
(Mt 19:9) And I say unto you, Whosoever shall put away his wife, except it be for fornicatic and shall marry another, commits adultery: and whoso marrieth her which is put away do⬛ commit adultery.
(1 Cor 6:12-20) All things are lawful for me, but not all things are profitable. All things a⬛ lawful for me, but I will not be mastered by anything. [13] Food is for the stomach and t⬛ stomach is for food, but God will do away with both of them Yet the body is not f⬛ immorality, but for the Lord, and the Lord is for the body. [14] Now God has not only rais⬛ the Lord, but will also raise us up through His power. [15] Do you not know that your bodi⬛ are members of Christ? Shall I then take away the members of Christ and make the⬛ members of a prostitute? May it never be! [16] Or do you not know that the one who joi⬛ himself to a prostitute is one body with her? For He says, "THE TWO SHALL BECOM⬛ ONE FLESH." [17] But the one who joins himself to the Lord is one spirit with Him. [1⬛ Flee immorality. Every other sin that a man commits is outside the body, but the immor⬛ man sins against his own body. [19] Or do you not know that your body is a temple of t⬛ Holy Spirit who is in you, whom you have from God, and that you are not your own? [2⬛ For you have been bought with a price: therefore glorify God in your body (NASB).
[4]
(2 Tim 2:21-22) If a man therefore purge himself from these, he shall be a vessel unto hono⬛ sanctified, and meet for the master's use, and prepared unto every good work. [22] Flee als⬛ youthful lusts: but follow righteousness, faith, charity, peace, with them that call on the Lor⬛ out of a pure heart.
[6]
(2 Cor 2:11) Lest Satan should get an advantage of us: for we are not ignorant of his devices.

1 THESSALONIANS 4:3-7

[4:3-7]
[3] For this is the will of God, even your sanctifycation, that you should abstain from fornication;
[4] That every one of you should know how to possess his vessel in sanctification and honor,
[5] Not in the lust of sensuality, even as the Gentiles who know not God;
[6] That no man go beyond and defraud his brother in any matter, because the Lord is the avenger of all such, as we also have forewarned you and testified.
[7] For God hath not called us unto uncleanness, but unto holiness.

The general term for sexual deviation of all kinds is **fornication** (πορνείας)(Mt 19:9; 1 Cor 6:12-20 [18]). The word often, however, is used more precisely of pre-marital failings. There is a touch of irony in this instruction. In the pagan world it was common for one consecrated to a god to perform deviant sexual activities. Paul's teachings were radical. Bruce notes, "This was a strange notion [abstinence] in the pagan society to which the gospel was first brought; there various forms of extra-marital sexual union were tolerated and some were even encouraged. A man might have a mistress who could provide him also with intellectual companionship; the institution of slavery made it easy for him to have a concubine, while casual gratification was readily available from a harlot." If God could demand abstinence of first century Christians, he also can of this generation.

[4] Verse four appears to be an elaboration of verse three and contrasts verse five. No small debate exists about this verse. The words **possess his vessel** (τὸ ἑαυτοῦ σκεῦος κτᾶσθαι) often receives much analysis. Note the options: *for each of you to know how to (acquire, possess) his own (vessel: wife, body) in sanctification....* The arguments, being voluminous, are difficult and taxing. The context appears to support the view that Paul urges **every one** to *take possession of* and preside over their **vessel** (i.e., person or body, 2 Tim 2:21-22). **But I deal severely with my body and bring it into subjection: lest... I myself should be a castaway** (1 Cor 9:27).

> If God could demand abstinence of century Christians,
> he also can of this generation.

[5] Negatively, we are not to preside over our body *in lustful passion* (NAB). The status quo of the licentious heathen (**the Gentiles**) is not deserving of emulation.

[6] One should take possession of his body in sanctification and honor so as to not **go beyond** (ὑπερβαίνειν) **and defraud** or *take advantage of* (πλεονεκτεῖν)(2 Cor 2:11) **his brother in** *this* (**any**) **matter**. Sexual sins are not victimless. Sexual purity within the church is in view. The existence of an **avenger** (ἔκδικος) serves as warning. It is **the Lord** who maintains law by discipline.

[7] The summons of the gospel is not to impure morals (**uncleanness**) but to consecration and holiness. Barclay notes, "One thing Christianity did was to lay down a completely new code in regard to the relationship of men and women; it is the champion of purity and the guardian of the home".

... 65 ...

GREEK TEXT

[8] τοιγαροῦν ὁ ἀθετῶν οὐκ ἄνθρωπον ἀθετεῖ ἀλλὰ τὸν θεὸν τὸν |omit| [UBS, καὶ] διδόντα τὸ πνεῦμα αὐτοῦ τὸ ἅγιον εἰς ὑμᾶς.

[9][π] Περὶ δὲ τῆς φιλαδελφίας οὐ χρείαν ἔχετε γράφειν ὑμῖν, αὐτοὶ γὰρ ὑμεῖς θεοδίδακτοί ἐστε εἰς τὸ ἀγαπᾶν ἀλλήλους· [10] καὶ γὰρ ποιεῖτε αὐτὸ εἰς πάντας τοὺς ἀδελφοὺς [τοὺς] ἐν ὅλῃ τῇ Μακεδονίᾳ. παρακαλοῦμεν

[π] δὲ ὑμᾶς, ἀδελφοί, περισσεύειν μᾶλλον, [11] καὶ φιλοτιμεῖσθαι ἡσυχάζειν καὶ πράσσειν τὰ ἴδια καὶ ἐργάζεσθαι ταῖς |omit| [UBS, ἰδίαις] χερσὶν ὑμῶν, καθὼς ὑμῖν παρηγγείλαμεν, [12] ἵνα περιπατῆτε εὐσχημόνως πρὸς τοὺς ἔξω καὶ μηδενὸς χρείαν ἔχητε.

REFERENCES

[11]

(Ro 15:20) Yea, so have I strived to preach the gospel, not where Christ was named, lest I should build upon another man's foundation:

(2 Cor 5:9-10) Wherefore we labor, that, whether present or absent, we may be accepted of him. [10] For we must all appear before the judgment seat of Christ; that every one may receive the things done in his body, according to that he hath done, whether it be good or bad.

(2 Thes 3:11) For we hear that there are some which walk among you disorderly, working not at all, but are busybodies.

[12]

(1 Cor 14:40) Let all things be done decently and in order.

(Ro 13:13) Let us walk honestly, as in the day; not in rioting and drunkenness, not in chambering and wantonness, not in strife and envying.

(Phil 4:19) But my God shall supply all your need according to his riches in glory by Christ Jesus.

There was no body of public opinion to discourage fornication. Bruce

[4:8-12]
[8] He therefore, that despiseth, despiseth not man but God who hath also given unto us his Holy Spirit.
[9][π] Now, as touching brotherly love, you need not that I write unto you; for you yourselves are taught of God to love one another.
[10a] And, indeed, you do it toward all the brethren who are in all Macedonia.
[10b][π] But we beseech you, brethren, that you increase more and more,
[11] And that you study to be quiet, and to do your own business, and to work with your own hands, as we commanded you,
[12] That you may walk honestly toward them that are outside, and that you may have lack of nothing.

[8] **He therefore** or *consequently* (τοιγαφοῦν), **the one despising** (*casting aside, violating*), **despises God**. The offence comes before God who has ownership and authority over the believer's body (1 Cor 6:19, **you are not your own....**). Because consecration is God's directive, those who fail to control themselves are in violation of God's standards. The **Holy Spirit** is elsewhere mentioned in similar contexts (1 Cor 6:18ff).

TOPIC # 2 LOVE

[9][π] A new topic begins (*Now, concerning....*). The term *concerning* (Πεφὶ) suggests that this issue is a response engendered by Timothy's report. The topic of **brotherly love** (φιλαδελφίας) receives "gentle reproof"- **you need not that I write unto you**. Eadie notes, "When God teaches (θεοδίδακτοί), the apostle may be silent".
[10a] Their exemplary behavior in **Macedonia** ends this discussion.

TOPIC # 3: BE INDUSTRIOUS

[10b][π] In the middle of this verse, another division begins. Verse divisions are completely arbitrary. *Now* (δὲ) we *exhort* **you brethren** begins this topic. The urging to *keep on, keeping on* is quite necessary in the growth of new converts.
[11] The first term **to study** means *to strive to* (φιλοτιμεῖσθαι)(Ro 15:20; 2 Cor 5:9-10). It modifies the other infinitives: *strive* **to be quiet** (ἡσυχάζειν), *to tend to your own affairs*, and **to work**. Noise is not the point of **being quiet**. It means to retain a calmness as opposed to unease or unrest (the opposite of 2 Thes 3:11). The third aim is to encourage the continuation of manual industry among the members (**work... hands**). This issue will resurface in 2 Thessalonians.
[12] The purpose of the preceding directives is to **walk honestly** or follow a benefiting scheme of life (εὐσχημόνως)(1 Cor 14:40; Ro 13:13). This speaks volumes to **them that are outside** (unbelievers). As a consequence of the aims of verse eleven, the believer will **have lack of nothing** (Phil 4:19).

GREEK TEXT

[13][π] Οὐ θέλομεν δὲ ὑμᾶς ἀγνοεῖν, ἀδελφοί, περὶ τῶν κοιμωμένων, ἵνα μὴ λυπῆσθε καθὼς καὶ οἱ λοιποὶ οἱ μὴ ἔχοντες ἐλπίδα. [14] εἰ γὰρ πιστεύομεν ὅτι Ἰησοῦς ἀπέθανεν καὶ ἀνέστη, οὕτως καὶ ὁ θεὸς τοὺς κοιμηθέντας διὰ τοῦ Ἰησοῦ ἄξει σὺν αὐτῷ. [15] Τοῦτο γὰρ ὑμῖν λέγομεν ἐν λόγῳ κυρίου, ὅτι ἡμεῖς οἱ ζῶντες οἱ περιλειπόμενοι εἰς τὴν παρουσίαν τοῦ κυρίου οὐ μὴ φθάσωμεν τοὺς κοιμηθέντας

REFERENCES

[13]
(1 Cor 10:1) Moreover, brethren, I would not that you should be ignorant, how that all our fathers were under the cloud, and all passed through the sea;
(1 Cor 12:1) Now concerning spiritual gifts, brethren, I would not have you ignorant.
(1 Cor 15:6, 18, 51) After that, he was seen of above five hundred brethren at once; of whom the greater part remain unto this present, but some are fallen asleep. [18] Then they also which are fallen asleep in Christ are perished. [51] Behold, I show you a mystery; We shall not all sleep, but we shall all be changed,
(2 Pt 3:4) And saying, Where is the promise of his coming? for since the fathers fell asleep, all things continue as they were from the beginning of the creation.
(1 Cor 15:18-19) Then they also which are fallen asleep in Christ are perished. [19] If in this life only we have hope in Christ, we are of all men most miserable.

All non-Pauline uses of **coming** or *parousia* in the N.T.

		Who is coming?	Text
MT	24:3	Lord Jesus Christ	What shall be the sign of your coming?
	24:27	Son of Man	For as the lightning cometh out of the East, and shines even unto the West: so shall also the coming of the Son of Man be.
	24:37	Son of Man	But as the days of Noah were, so shall also the coming of the Son of Man be.
	24:39	Son of Man	And knew not until the flood came, and took them away; so shall also the coming of the Son of Man be.
James	5:7	The Lord	Be patient... unto the coming of the Lord.
	5:8	The Lord	... for the coming of the Lord draweth nigh.
2 Peter	1:16	Lord Jesus Christ	For we have not followed cunningly devised fables, when we made known unto you the power and coming of our Lord Jesus Christ.
	3:4	Lord Jesus Christ	Where is the promise of his coming? for since the fathers fell asleep, all things continue as they were from the beginning of the creation.
	3:12	the Day of God	Looking for... the coming of the day of God, wherein the heavens being on fire shall be dissolved....
1 John	2:28	Lord Jesus Christ	... abide in him; that, when he shall appear we may have confidence and not be ashamed before him at his coming.

1 THESSALONIANS 4:13-15

TOPIC # 4: THOSE SLEEPING

[4:13-15]
[13][π] But I would not have you to be ignorant, brethren, concerning them who are asleep, that you sorrow not, even as others who have no hope. [14] For if we believe that Jesus died and rose again, even so them also who sleep in Jesus will God bring with him. [15] For this we say unto you by the word of the Lord, that we who are alive and remain unto the coming of the Lord shall not prevent them who are asleep.

[13][π] **But** or *now,* as in vv 9 and 10b, indicates a new topic. The **I** is better *we* (θέλομεν). The introductory formula *we* **would not have you to be ignorant, brethren**.... occurs elsewhere (1 Cor 10:1, 12:1), suggesting the note worthiness of the instruction. The realm of discussion: **concerning them who are asleep.** Greater detail follows, aiding in reconstructing the points of difficulty. Those who are **asleep** are those who are dead. The term **asleep** (κοιμωμένων) has been used in antiquity as a euphemistic substitute referring to those that have died (1 Cor 15:6, 18, 51; 2 Pt 3:4). The purpose of this discussion is clearly indicated- **that you sorrow not** (ἵνα μὴ λυπῆσθε, *stop sorrowing*). The added comment, **even as others who have no hope**, exposes the inappro-priateness of their grieving. Grieving and efforts in behalf of the departed is not limited to the ancient world. **Hope** (ἐλπίδα) speaks of certainty in the N.T., not as it is commonly understood today (1 Cor 15:18-19). Hope is not a gamble.

[14] Verse fourteen gives the foundational reason (**for,** γάρ) to spurn the grief that began. The resurrection of **Jesus** is the assurance of the resurrection of those **who sleep in Jesus. God** *shall* **bring** (ἄξει) **with him** *those who have slept.* They will take part in that glorious meeting in the air: the rapture.

[15] The **for** (γάρ), beginning this verse, is more introductory than a reasoning of information. The grounds on which the issue is placed- **the word of the Lord.** *Those living, remaining* **unto the** *visitation* (**coming,** *parousia*) **of the Lord** *will* not *precede those who have slept* (i.e., died). The exact meaning and nuances of **prevent** (φθάσωμεν) in this context are not found without effort. Some take it as *to go before* (Louw/Nida), others as *precede* (Findlay), *antic-ipate* (Frame), and even *have advantage over* (Wanamaker). Bruce states, "The verb [**prevent**] (2:16) means to anticipate someone in doing something. Presumably the Thessalonian Christians had wondered if those of their number who had died would suffer any disadvantage through not being alive to witness the Parousia and participate in its attendant glory." The force of this last statement resides in a double negative (οὐ μή); an advantage *WILL NOT* occur.

The particle δὲ (postpositive conjunction) is often used in Pauline literature as a transitional particle translated, **Now**.... It is a highly definitive marker, signaling the author's divisions.

... 69 ...

GREEK TEXT

[16] ὅτι αὐτὸς ὁ κύριος ἐν κελεύσματι, ἐν φωνῇ ἀρχαγγέλου καὶ ἐν σάλπιγγι θεοῦ, καταβήσεται ἀπ' οὐρανοῦ, καὶ οἱ νεκροὶ ἐν Χριστῷ ἀναστήσονται πρῶτον, [17] ἔπειτα ἡμεῖς οἱ ζῶντες οἱ περιλειπόμενοι ἅμα σὺν αὐτοῖς ἁρπαγησόμεθα ἐν νεφέλαις εἰς ἀπάντησιν τοῦ κυρίου εἰς ἀέρα· καὶ οὕτως πάντοτε σὺν κυρίῳ ἐσόμεθα. [18] Ὥστε παρακαλεῖτε ἀλλήλους ἐν τοῖς λόγοις τούτοις.

REFERENCES

[16]

(Rev 4:1) After this I looked, and, behold, a door was opened in heaven: and the first voice which I heard was as it were of a trumpet talking with me; which said, Come up hither, and I will show you things which must be hereafter.

(2 Cor 5:1-5) For we know that if our earthly house of this tabernacle were dissolved, we have a building of God, an house not made with hands, eternal in the heavens. [2] For in this we groan, earnestly desiring to be clothed upon with our house which is from heaven: [3] If so be that being clothed we shall not be found naked. [4] For we that are in this tabernacle do groan, being burdened: not for that we would be unclothed, but clothed upon, that mortality might be swallowed up of life. [5] Now he that hath wrought us for the selfsame thing is God, who also hath given unto us the earnest of the Spirit.

(1 Cor 15:22ff) For as in Adam all die, even so in Christ shall all be made alive. [23] But every man in his own order: Christ the first fruits; afterward they that are Christ's at his coming. [24] Then cometh the end, when he shall have delivered up the kingdom to God, even the Father; when he shall have put down all rule and all authority and power.

[17]

(Mt 25:6) And at midnight there was a cry made, Behold, the bridegroom cometh; go out to meet him.

[4:16-18]
[16] For the Lord himself shall descend from heaven with a shout, with the voice of the archangel, and with the trump of God; and the dead in Christ shall rise first; [17] Then we who are alive and remain shall be caught up together with them in the clouds to meet the Lord in the air; and so shall we ever be with the Lord. [18] Wherefore, comfort one another with these words.

[16] There are three audible signs: **a shout, the voice,** and the **trump of God.** The **shout** (κελεύσματι) is a military term like an order. It may be that **the voice of the archangel** issues the shout and it is as **the trump** (σάλπιγγι) **of God** (Rev 4:1). **In a moment, in the twinkling of an eye, at the last trump, for the trumpet shall sound, and the dead shall be raised incorruptible, and we shall be changed** (1 Cor 15:52). How can **the dead in Christ rise first** if God brings those with him who have slept (v 14)? Those who die are present with the Lord (2 Cor 5:1-5) yet do not experience a resurrected body until their "order" of resurrection (1 Cor 15:22ff). The relationship of **first, then,** (v 17) is instructive. The resurrection of sleeping saints **(the dead in Christ)** and the meeting **in the air** distinguish the rapture from the second advent.
[17] When Paul speaks of **we** it is defined as *those living, remaining* (οἱ περιλειπόμενοι)(v 15), not necessarily of himself and others living in his day. Paul did not know the when of His coming, neither do we! Note the word order as it relates to the issue, *we the living ones, remaining, together with them we shall be snatched....* This "phrase gives the most precise statement of the equality of advantage that we have" (Frame). Some take **together** (ἅμα) in the sense of *simultaneously.* The meeting place: **in the clouds in the air. To meet,** is literally, *unto a meeting of the Lord....* This *meeting* (ἀπάντησιν) is one of anticipation and jubilation (Mt 25:6). It should be observed that this scheme of resurrection is harmonious with 1 Cor 15:22-24a, **For just as in Adam all are dieing, so also in Christ all shall be made alive, but each according to his own order, Christ the first fruits** (v 14), **then those of Christ at his coming** (*parousia,* vv 14-17), **Then the end when....** This event, called the rapture comes from the word **caught** (Lat., *rapere*). It implies a sudden irresistible force, similar to Enoch being snatched away **(for God took him,** Gn 5:24). The final clause reads, *and thus always with the Lord we shall be!*
[18] **Wherefore** (Ὥστε) draws the discussion toward an application. Now informed, not ignorant (v 13), they are commanded to comfort one another (not sorrow, v 13) **with these words.** Paul does not simply offer encouragement but binds each of them to the task. Perhaps the best translation of **comfort** (παρακαλεῖτε) in this context is *to console* (Lat., *consolamini*). Sound doctrine gives comfort and calm to believers who reside in a world of chaos and hopelessness.

GREEK TEXT

[18] Ὥστε παρακαλεῖτε ἀλλήλους ἐν τοῖς λόγοις τούτοις.

[1][π] Περὶ δὲ τῶν χρόνων καὶ τῶν καιρῶν, ἀδελφοί, οὐ χρείαν ἔχετε ὑμῖν γράφεσθαι, [2] αὐτοὶ γὰρ ἀκριβῶς οἴδατε ὅτι ἡμέρα κυρίου ὡς κλέπτης ἐν νυκτὶ οὕτως ἔρχεται. [3] ὅταν λέγωσιν, Εἰρήνη καὶ ἀσφάλεια, τότε αἰφνίδιος αὐτοῖς ἐφίσταται ὄλεθρος ὥσπερ ἡ ὠδὶν τῇ ἐν γαστρὶ ἐχούσῃ, καὶ οὐ μὴ ἐκφύγωσιν.

REFERENCES

[2]

(Mt 24:36) But of that day and hour no man knows, no, not the angels of heaven, but my Father only.
(Amos 5:18-20) Woe unto you that desire the day of the LORD! to what end is it for you? the day of the LORD is darkness, and not light. [19] As if a man did flee from a lion, and a bear met him; or went into the house, and leaned his hand on the wall, and a serpent bit him. [20] Shall not the day of the LORD be darkness, and not light? even very dark, and no brightness in it?
(Isa 13:6-16) Howl ye; for the day of the LORD is at hand; it shall come as a destruction from the Almighty. [7] Therefore shall all hands be faint, and every man's heart shall melt: [8] And they shall be afraid: pangs and sorrows shall take hold of them; they shall be in pain as a woman that travails: they shall be amazed one at another; their faces shall be as flames. [9] Behold, the day of the LORD cometh, cruel both with wrath and fierce anger, to lay the land desolate: and he shall destroy the sinners thereof out of it. [10] For the stars of heaven and the constellations thereof shall not give their light: the sun shall be darkened in his going forth, and the moon shall not cause her light to shine. [11] And I will punish the world for their evil, and the wicked for their iniquity; and I will cause the arrogancy of the proud to cease, and will lay low the haughtiness of the terrible. [12] I will make a man more precious than fine gold; even a man than the golden wedge of Ophir. [13] Therefore I will shake the heavens, and the earth shall remove out of her place, in the wrath of the LORD of hosts, and in the day of his fierce anger. [14] And it shall be as the chased roe, and as a sheep that no man takes up: they shall every man turn to his own people, and flee every one into his own land. [15] Every one that is found shall be thrust through; and every one that is joined unto them shall fall by the sword. [16] Their children also shall be dashed to pieces before their eyes; their houses shall be spoiled, and their wives ravished.
(Jl 1:15) Alas for the day! for the day of the LORD is at hand, and as a destruction from the Almighty shall it come.
(Ob 15-21) For the day of the LORD is near upon all the heathen....
(Zech 14:1-4a) Behold, the day of the LORD cometh, and thy spoil shall be divided in the midst of thee. [2] For I will gather all nations against Jerusalem to battle; and the city shall be taken, and the houses rifled, and the women ravished; and half of the city shall go forth into captivity, and the residue of the people shall not be cut off from the city. [3] Then shall the LORD go forth, and fight against those nations, as when he fought in the day of battle. [4] And his feet shall stand in that day upon the mount of Olives
(Phil 1:10) That you may approve things that are excellent; that ye may be sincere and without offence till the day of Christ. (Phil 2:16) Holding forth the word of life; that I may rejoice in the day of Christ
[3]
(Ez 13:10-16) Because, even because they have seduced my people, saying, Peace; and there was no peace; and one built up a wall, and, lo, others daubed it with untempered morter: [11] Say unto them which daub it with untempered morter, that it shall fall: there shall be an overflowing shower; and ye, O great hailstones, shall fall; and a stormy wind shall rend it.... [13] Therefore thus saith the Lord GOD; I will even rend it with a stormy wind in my fury; and there shall be an overflowing shower in mine anger, and great hailstones in my fury to consume it. [14] So will I break down the wall that ye have daubed with untempered morter, and bring it down to the ground, so that the foundation thereof shall be discovered, and it shall fall, and ye shall be consumed in the midst thereof: and ye shall know that I am the LORD. [15] Thus will I accomplish my wrath upon the wall, and upon them that have daubed it with untempered morter, and will say unto you, The wall is no more, neither they that daubed it; [16] To wit, the prophets of Israel which prophesy concerning Jerusalem, and which see visions of peace for her, and there is no peace, saith the Lord GOD.
(Jer 6:14) They have healed also the hurt of the daughter of my people slightly, saying, Peace, peace; when there is no peace.

TOPIC # 5: OF THE TIMES AND SEASONS

[5:1-3]
[1][π] But of the times and the seasons, brethren you have no need that I write unto you. [2] For yourselves know perfectly that the day of the Lord so comes as a thief in the night. [3] For when they shall say, Peace and safety, then sudden destruction cometh upon them, as travail upon a woman with child, and they shall not escape.

[1][π] **But** or *now* (δὲ)... **brethren,** indicates a different issue begins. **Times and seasons** may be understood as *durations and occasions.* These "'whens' "refer respectively to the length of time that will pass (*chronoi*) and the special character of the divinely appointed moments (*kairoi*) when God acts." (Frame). Paul again deems the topic only as a repetition (4:9), not really necessary to **write** on. Thankfully, he does address this issue. [2] Verse two completes the start of verse one. **For** (γὰρ) begins the reason that **no need** to **write** exists: **yourselves know....** They know *accurately*, or *precisely* (ἀκριβῶς), **that the day of the Lord as a thief in the night** *thus* **comes.** The answer to the date of the Day of the Lord is that there is no answer (Mt 24:36). The simile (**as,** ὡς) vividly tells that as no one can anticipate a thief, so no one can predict the beginning of **the day of the Lord.** Thieves do not call ahead. This special phrase, **the day of the Lord,** is found in the O.T. (Amos 5:18-20; Isa 13:6-16; Jl 1:15; Ob 15-21; Zech 14) and is developed more specifically in the N.T. (ἡμέρα κυρίου, Phil 1:10, 2:16; 2 Pt 3:1-10). Bruce says it is "the day when Yahweh would vindicate his righteous cause and execute impartial judgment". The events of the day include the rapture, Antichrist's signing of the covenant, the tribulation period, Armageddon, the second advent, the millennial kingdom, and the abolition of the earth and heavens that be. Paul had taught the young believers of Thessalonica concerning the end times (Eschatology).

The plainness, simplicity and picturesque clarity of **as a thief in the night** has routinely been invalidated by the foolishness of untrustworthy men.

[3] **When they** *might* **say peace and** *security* (ἀσφάλεια) typifies the sense of calm before the cataclysm of **the day.** Ezekiel reveals the lesson of the **sudden destruction- And you will know that I am the LORD** (Ez 13:10-16; Jer 6:14). Christians, taken at the rapture, will be rescued from these events (1:10). Note the pronouns: **they... them... they... But YOU, brethren** (v 4). The second simile (**as,** ὥσπερ) illustrates the unavoidable and sudden circumstances of the day, using a woman in labor. The surprise of birth pangs begins the inescapable difficulties of labor. The terrifying state of affairs for the wicked is such that there is absolutely (οὐ μὴ) no **escape.**

GREEK TEXT

[4] ὑμεῖς δέ, ἀδελφοί, οὐκ ἐστὲ ἐν σκότει, ἵνα ἡ ἡμέρα ὑμᾶς ὡς |κλέπτης| [UBS, κλέπτας] καταλάβῃ, [5] πάντες γὰρ ὑμεῖς υἱοὶ φωτός ἐστε καὶ υἱοὶ ἡμέρας. οὐκ ἐσμὲν νυκτὸς οὐδὲ σκότους· [6] ἄρα οὖν μὴ καθεύδωμεν ὡς οἱ λοιποί, ἀλλὰ γρηγορῶμεν καὶ νήφωμεν. [7] οἱ γὰρ καθεύδοντες νυκτὸς καθεύδουσιν, καὶ οἱ μεθυσκόμενοι νυκτὸς μεθύουσιν· [8] ἡμεῖς δὲ ἡμέρας ὄντες νήφωμεν, ἐνδυσάμενοι θώρακα πίστεως καὶ ἀγάπης καὶ περικεφαλαίαν ἐλπίδα σωτηρίας·

REFERENCES

[4]
(Ro 1:21-22) Because that, when they knew God, they glorified him not as God, neither were thankful; but became vain in their imaginations, and their foolish heart was darkened. [22] Professing themselves to be wise, they became fools,
(Ro 2:19) And art confident that thou thyself art a guide of the blind, a light of them which are in darkness,
(1 Cor 4: 5) Therefore judge nothing before the time, until the Lord come, who both will bring to light the hidden things of darkness, and will make manifest the counsels of the hearts: and then shall every man have praise of God.
[5]
(Jn 1:4-5) In him was life; and the life was the light of men. [5] And the light shineth in darkness; and the darkness comprehended it not.
(2 Cor 4:4) In whom the god of this world hath blinded the minds of them which believe not, lest the light of the glorious gospel of Christ, who is the image of God, should shine unto them.
[6]
(Mt 24:43) But know this, that if the good man of the house had known in what watch the thief would come, he would have watched, and would not have suffered his house to be broken up.
[8]
(Eph 6:10-18) Finally, my brethren, be strong in the Lord, and in the power of his might. [11] Put on the whole armor of God, that ye may be able to stand against the wiles of the devil. [12] For we wrestle not against flesh and blood, but against principalities, against powers, against the rulers of the darkness of this world, against spiritual wickedness in high places. [13] Wherefore take unto you the whole armor of God, that ye may be able to withstand in the evil day, and having done all, to stand. [14] Stand therefore, having your loins girt about with truth, and having on the breastplate of righteousness; [15] And your feet shod with the preparation of the gospel of peace; [16] Above all, taking the shield of faith, wherewith you shall be able to quench all the fiery darts of the wicked. [17]   A n d take the helmet of salvation, and the sword of the Spirit, which is the word of God: [18] Praying always with all prayer and supplication in the Spirit, and watching thereunto with all perseverance and supplication for all saints;
(Isa 59:18-20) According to their deeds, accordingly he will repay, fury to his adversaries, recompense to his enemies; to the islands he will repay recompense. [19] So shall they fear the name of the LORD from the west, and his glory from the rising of the sun. When the enemy shall come in like a flood, the Spirit of the LORD shall lift up a standard against him. [20] And the Redeemer shall come to Zion, and unto them that turn from transgression in Jacob, saith the LORD.

It's not in the numbers.

[5:4-8]
[4] But you, brethren, are not in darkness, that that day should overtake you as a thief.
[5] For you are all sons of light, and sons of the day; we are not of the night nor of darkness.
[6] Therefore, let us not sleep, as do others, but let us watch and be sober.
[7] For they that sleep sleep in the night; and they that are drunk are drunk in the night.
[8] But let us, who are of the day, be sober, putting on the breastplate of faith and love, and for an helmet, the hope of salvation.

[4] A change of subject: **But YOU** (emphatic, ὑμεῖς δέ) **brethren**. It seems possible that **in darkness** may be figurative of *in ignorance* (Ro 1:21-22, 2:19; 1 Cor 4:5). We speak of those 'who are in the dark'. More likely it tells of the spiritual realm believers are not a part of. Enlightened, anticipating, and absent from the realm of spiritual darkness, the believers will not be **overtaken** (καταλάβῃ) **as a thief** (v 2) by **that day**.
[5] Verse five gives the reason (**For**) that that day will not overtake the believer: we are **sons of light** (φωτός). This phrase speaks of those who are in union with Jesus, **the Light of the world** (Jn 1:4-5; 2 Cor 4:4).
[6] This verse is "what reason and duty both demand" (Frame). **Therefore** (ἄρα οὖν) begins a conclusion in the form of three exhortations. These are: **let us not sleep, let us watch, and let us be sober.** The first admonition prohibits moral indolence (*slumber*). **And that, knowing the time, that now it is high time to awake out of sleep: for now is our salvation nearer than when we believed** (Ro 13:11). This verb **sleep** (καθεύδωμεν) is not the same word as in 4:13. The **others** is literally *the rest* (i.e., the unsaved), as in 4:13, **who are having no hope**. Positively, to **watch** (γρηγορῶμεν) is to remain alert to action (Mt 24:43; Rev 16:15), while to **be sober** (≠ non drunk)(νήφωμεν) denotes ethical and moral restraints necessary for an effective role of vigilance.
[7] This verse is a truism– a self evident truth. It seems to function as a contrast to the activities admonished in verse six.
[8] **But us** (ἡμεῖς δὲ), contrasting verse seven, **let us be sober**. Again, the encouragement to **be sober** (νήφωμεν), but here it is elaborated on. The vigilance encouraged is that of **putting on** the "armor of light". The articles of armor, numbering two, fall short of those listed in Ephesians 6:10-18. It may be that they are inspired by the text of Isaiah 59:17, **And he put on righteousness like a breastplate, And a helmet of salvation on His head; And he put on garments of vengeance for clothing, And wrapped himself with zeal as a mantle.** It seems that by design, Paul uses this text in Isaiah which refers to the second advent of Christ's return (Isa 59:18-20). The **breastplate** (θώρακα) **and helmet** (περικεφαλαίαν) constitute the necessary armor securing the vital organs. With **faith**, **love**, and the certain **hope** generated by **salvation**, the believer is outfitted for more than just survival in his spiritual warfare.

It's not in the 6rln3m5e7s4b2u.

GREEK TEXT

[9] ὅτι οὐκ ἔθετο ἡμᾶς ὁ θεὸς εἰς ὀργὴν ἀλλὰ εἰς περιποίησιν σωτηρίας διὰ τοῦ κυρίου ἡμῶν Ἰησοῦ Χριστοῦ, [10] τοῦ ἀποθανόντος |ὑπὲρ| [UBS, περὶ] ἡμῶν ἵνα εἴτε γρηγορῶμεν εἴτε καθεύδωμεν ἅμα σὺν αὐτῷ ζήσωμεν. [11] Διὸ παρακαλεῖτε ἀλλή-λους καὶ οἰκοδομεῖτε εἰς τὸν ἕνα, καθὼς καὶ ποιεῖτε.

REFERENCES

[9]

(1 Pet 2:9) But you are a chosen generation, a royal priesthood, an holy nation, a peculiar people; that you should show forth the praises of him who hath called you out of darkness into his marvelous light;

(Eph 1:14) Which is the earnest of our inheritance until the redemption of the purchased possession, unto the praise of his glory.

[11]

(1 Cor 14:4) He that speaks in an unknown tongue edifies himself; but he that prophesies edifies the church.

[5:9-11]
[9] For God hath not appointed us to wrath but to obtain salvation by our Lord Jesus Christ, [10] Who died for us that, whether we wake or sleep, we should live together with him. [11] Wherefore, comfort yourselves together, and edify one another, even as also you do.

[9] The word **for** begins a verse in this section for the fifth time. Supported instruction saturates this topic. Paul assures them of their ultimate protection in their advance. God's **wrath** in the day of the Lord will not touch those dying in Christ or those believers living at his coming (1:10). Conversely (ἀλλά, **but**), we are *placed* (ἔθετο, **appointed**) *unto* an acquisition of **salvation by our Lord Jesus Christ** (1 Pt 2:9). [10] **Who died** is the Lord Jesus of verse nine. His death secures the believer's life! A more literal translation might be, *who died in our behalf in order that we might live together with him, whether we might be watchful, whether we might slumber.* Although some take **sleep** (καθεύδωμεν) as death, the Greek word is different than in 4:13-18 (κοιμωμένων) and warrants no different meaning in this context. Those believers who are vigilant or not will one day **live together** with the one who died in their behalf.

[11] **Wherefore** (Διό) is a term that funnels previous information into an application, command or statement. Based on the information given, **comfort** *one another* (παρακαλεῖτε ἀλλήλους). This topic requires a similar activity as the last issue- **comfort** (4:18). They should not stop there. **Edify** (οἰκοδομεῖτε, 1 Cor 14:4) is a construction term meaning to build up as opposed to tearing down. They are directed to become active laborers in the building of their fellow brothers and sisters in Christ. Again Paul cites the active faith among the Thessalonians -**even as also you do.**

The next section is the last major section of the body. It is called the Parenesis referring to exhortations, usually in the form of commands.

Distribution of Commands		
OPENING	Prescript / Exordium	0
BODY	Narratio / Prayer Wish	0
	Topics	3
	Parenesis / Prayer Wish	15
CLOSING	Post Script	2

GREEK TEXT

[12][π] Ἐρωτῶμεν δὲ ὑμᾶς, ἀδελφοί, εἰδέναι τοὺς κοπιῶντας ἐν ὑμῖν καὶ προϊσταμένους ὑμῶν ἐν κυρίῳ καὶ νουθετοῦντας ὑμᾶς, [13] καὶ ἡγεῖσθαι αὐτοὺς
ὑπερεκπερισσοῦ ἐν ἀγάπῃ διὰ τὸ ἔργον αὐτῶν. εἰρηνεύετε ἐν ἑαυτοῖς. [14]
παρακαλοῦμεν δὲ ὑμᾶς, ἀδελφοί, νουθετεῖτε τοὺς ἀτάκτους, παραμυθεῖσθε τοὺς
ὀλιγοψύχους, ἀντέχεσθε τῶν ἀσθενῶν, μακροθυμεῖτε πρὸς πάντας.

REFERENCES

[12]

(Phil 1:1) Paul and Timothy, the servants of Jesus Christ, to all the saints in Christ Jesus
which are at Philippi, with the bishops and deacons:

(Titus 1:5) For this cause left I thee in Crete, that you should set in order the things that are
wanting, and ordain elders in every city, as I had appointed thee:

(1 Tim 3:4) One that rules well his own house, having his children in subjection with all
gravity;

[14]

(Ro 12:1) I beseech you therefore, brethren, by the mercies of God, that ye present your
bodies a living sacrifice, holy, acceptable unto God, which is your reasonable service.

(Gal 5:22) But the fruit of the Spirit is love, joy, peace, longsuffering, gentleness, goodness,
faith,

(1 Cor 13:4) Charity suffers long, and is kind; charity envies not; charity vaunts not itself, is
not puffed up,

*Verses twelve through twenty-four constitute
the parenesis of the letter. This section is the last major
section of the body. This group of commands
is very rich in form and application.*

[5:12-14]
[12][π] And we be-
seech you, brethren,
to know them who
labor among you,
and are over you in
the Lord, and ad-
monish you.
[13] And to esteem
them very highly in
love for their work's
sake. *And* be at peace
among yourselves.
[14][π] Now we ex-
hort you, brethren,
warn them that are
unruly, encourage
the fainthearted,
support the weak,
be patient toward all
men.

[12][π] *Now* (δὲ, **And?**) we *ask* (Ἐρωτῶμεν, **beseech**) **you brethren**… starts the division. Paul first requests appreciation for leaders. The fact that those leading have no titles again corroborates the historical situation of Paul's short stay in Thessalonica (Phil 1:1; Titus 1:5). Having been removed from the city in haste, the appointment of elders was not completed. The first admonition is to **know** or *recognize* (εἰδέναι) those leading. Those leading constitute one group and are distinguished by function: they **labor** (κοπιῶντας), **are over you** (προϊσταμένους, 1 Tim 3:4), and are **admonishing** or *advising* **you** (νουθετοῦντας, 5:14). In these three activities–labor, leading, and counsel, we find a valuable set of responsibilities in ministry life. **In the Lord** relates their sphere of spiritual leadership.

[13] The second admonition is to **esteem** or *regard* (ἡγεῖσθαι) **them** *abundantly* (ὑπερεκπερισσοῦ) **in love**. Why? *Because of* **their work**. Appropriate appreciation sums up vv 12-13. *And* is italicized because of its unnecessary addition. The order for **peace** (εἰρηνεύετε) clearly targets unity. To live in concord among the brethren and with those in authority, one must make peace his close friend and conflict his unwelcome guest.

[14][π] *Now* (δὲ), **we exhort** (παρακαλοῦμεν, Ro 12:1) **you, brethren**… starts a division. Paul next encourages responsibilities to other believers: The first of three directives orders believers to **warn the unruly**. **Warn** (νουθετεῖτε) comes from two Greek words meaning *to place to the mind*. Our word nouthetic comes from it. It involves blame and instruction. Those in need of warning are *those not in their appointed place* (ἀτάκτους). The term **unruly** is a military word for those out of order regarding their duties. Some see the term denoting only laziness. Although that can be a part of unruly, the term is general (2 Thes 3:6-15). The disobedient must be confronted with their disobedience to Christ. The second, **encourage** (παραμυθεῖσθε) **the fainthearted**, speaks of helping those who are despondent, exasperated, or discouraged in their walk of faith. Literally rendered, *little souls* (ὀλιγοψύχους) expresses "those whose hearts are not

GREEK TEXT

[14][π] παρακαλοῦμεν δὲ ὑμᾶς, ἀδελφοί, νουθετεῖτε τοὺς ἀτάκτους, παραμυθεῖσθε τοὺς ὀλιγοψύχους, ἀντέχεσθε τῶν ἀσθενῶν, μακροθυμεῖτε πρὸς πάντας.

[15][π] ὁρᾶτε μή τις κακὸν ἀντὶ κακοῦ τινι ἀποδῷ, ἀλλὰ πάντοτε τὸ ἀγαθὸν διώκετε Ικαὶ [UBS, omit] εἰς ἀλλήλους καὶ εἰς πάντας.

REFERENCES

[14]

(Ro 12:1) I beseech you therefore, brethren, by the mercies of God, that you present your bodies a living sacrifice, holy, acceptable unto God, which is your reasonable service.

(Gal 5:22) But the fruit of the Spirit is love, joy, peace, longsuffering, gentleness, goodness, faith,

(1 Cor 13:4) Charity suffers long, and is kind; charity envies not; charity vaunts not itself, is not puffed up,

[15]

(1 Cor 14:1) Follow after charity, and desire spiritual gifts, but rather that you may prophesy.

1.D, 2.B, 3.A, 4.C

[5:14-15]
[14][π] Now we ex-
hort you, brethren,
warn them that are
unruly, encourage
the fainthearted,
support the weak,
be patient toward all
men.
[15][π] See that none
render evil for evil
unto any man, but
ever follow that
which is good, both
among yourselves,
and to all men.

strong" (Frame). The distraught must be encouraged in their walk with Christ. The third, **support the weak**, means to *stand by* or *prop up* (ἀντέχεσθε) those who are spiritually weak (ἀσθενῶν). The unable must be aided in their walk with Christ. It should be understood what a grievous error it would be to mismatch these actions and recipients. For instance, to approach the weak confrontationally. At this point, "Paul seems to turn from the specific needs of the three classes just named to a need of the group as a whole in reference to one another...." (**be patient**....). "Patience is a fruit of the Spirit (Ga 5:22) and a characteristic of love (1 Cor 13:4, **Love is patient**)" (Frame). The word patience (μακροθυμεῖτε) itself denotes *slow to passion* or *anger*- a posture hardly disposable in the edifying relationships of believers.

Are we our brother's keepers?

[15][π] Paul now warns against vindictiveness: **see** or *beware, watch out* (ὁρᾶτε), **that none render evil for evil**.... This command, contrasting the former, prohibits the 'get even' lifestyle that characterizes mankind. It tells us that one responds to being wronged not by doing wrong in return. In contrast (**but**, *on the contrary*), *always* (**ever follow**) *pursue* (διώκετε, 1 Cor 14:1) *the good unto one another and unto all* (*love is genuine, abhorring the evil– being joined to the good*, Ro 12:9). The scope of this directive is not just among the brethren, but **to all**– including unbelievers. We are our brother's keepers.

Using vv 14-15, Match the Biblical Action to the Appropriate Recipient.	
1. ___ Encourage	A. Everyone
2. ___ Prop Up	B. The Weak
3. ___ Be Patient	C. Disobedient Ones
4. ___ Confront	D. The Distraught

GREEK TEXT

[16][π] Πάντοτε χαίρετε, [17] ἀδιαλείπτως προσεύχεσθε, [18] ἐν παντὶ εὐχαριστεῖτε: τοῦτο γὰρ θέλημα θεοῦ ἐν Χριστῷ Ἰησοῦ εἰς ὑμᾶς.

REFERENCES

[16]

(Jn 11:35) Jesus wept (ἐδάκρυσεν ὁ Ἰησοῦς).

[18]

(Ro 1:21) Because that, when they knew God, they glorified him not as God, neither were thankful; but became vain in their imaginations, and their foolish heart was darkened.

(Col 2:7) Rooted and built up in him, and stablished in the faith, as you have been taught, abounding therein with thanksgiving.

[EXCURSUS]

"Popular Misconceptions"

"By far the most prevalent of the inadequate and misleading claims of popular exegesis is that the present imperative with μὴ means 'stop' doing something that is already being done, and the corollary to it, although not so commonly insisted upon nor stated, says that the aorist prohibition (μὴ with the aorist subjunctive) means 'don't start' doing something that is not yet being done. The 'rule' is used to prove such statements to the effect that the Christians at Ephesus were continuing to be thieves and drunkards (Eph 4:26, 5:18)".

[Eph 4:26] Be ye angry, and sin not: let not the sun go down upon your wrath:

[Eph 5:18] And be not drunk with wine, wherein is excess; but be filled with the Spirit.

"Many of the beginning and intermediate grammars present this inadequate and misleading concept, often without any suggestion that it is true only part of the time".

(*Grace Theological Journal*, spring 87, vol. 8 #1, p.42)

[5:16-18]
[16][π] Rejoice
evermore.
[17] Pray without
ceasing.
[18] In everything
give thanks; for this
is the will of God in
Christ Jesus
concerning you.

[16] Verses 16-18 are a unit, expressing the believer's personal responsibilities. Hendrickson calls vv 16-18, "Three beautiful, closely related, and tersely expressed admonitions". **Rejoice in the Lord always, again I say rejoice!** (Phil 4:4). The author defines rejoicing as the soul's response to peace with God. We are to *always* (Πάντοτε) *be rejoicing*. It may be trivial to point out that this is the shortest verse in the New Testament– in Greek (14 letters)(Jn 11:35, 16 letters).

[17] It is surprising that this command is so widely misunderstood. Many, without warrant or grounds, modify this command to say 'Be in the spirit of prayer'. A search for the phrase "spirit of prayer" retrieves "No Results". Had Paul wanted to say "Be in....", he would have! See FIG 1. To **pray** means to offer requests to God. To pray **without ceasing** indicates not duration of time but manner. We are to pray *repeatedly* (ἀδιαλείπτως), not repetitiously. This adverb was used in antiquity of paying taxes, coughing, the production of fruit, and of a fortress that was repeatedly attacked. These contexts illustrate HOW (not when) we are to pray: with persistent regularity. One must continue to ask to receive an answer. There are many easy applications for this directive, such as praying at the beginning of each hour.

[18] "Ingratitude is one of the features of pagan depravity in Ro 1:21: the children of God are expected to 'abound in thanksgiving'" (Bruce, Col 2:7). Hendrickson states, "When a person prays without giving thanks, he has clipped the wings of prayer, so that it cannot rise." *In all circumstances* (**in everything**) of life, we are to offer our thanks to God. The gift of life and the gift of life with Christ hereafter is substance enough for thanksgiving. Again **the will of God** is something to be practiced, not groped for (4:3).

[Excursus: These lines are often the victim of 'mirror reading': the view that if something is prohibited, there must be an actual problem in or among the recipients. For example, Heibert notes on v 20, "This verse makes it clear that some members of the Thessalonian church had a low evaluation of prophesying. Obviously some local circumstances had brought it into disrepute". This view seems to contradict the favorable evaluation Paul has articulated (1:3, 7, 8; 2:14; 3:6. [GTJ, spring 87, vol. 8 #1]

FIG 1
What Paul **DID NOT** write:
ἴσθι ἐν τῷ πνεύματι τῆς προσευχῆς
[*Be in the spirit of prayer.*]

What Paul **DID** write:
ἀδιαλείπτως προσεύχεσθε
[*Pray repeatedly.*]

GREEK TEXT

[19][π] τὸ πνεῦμα μὴ σβέννυτε, [20] προφητείας μὴ ἐξουθενεῖτε· [21] πάντα δὲ δοκιμάζετε, τὸ καλὸν κατέχετε, [22] ἀπὸ παντὸς εἴδους πονηροῦ ἀπέχεσθε.

REFERENCES

[19]

(Ac 2:2-4) And suddenly there came a sound from heaven as of a rushing mighty wind, and it filled all the house where they were sitting. [3] And there appeared unto them cloven tongues like as of fire, and it sat upon each of them. [4] And they were all filled with the Holy Ghost, and began to speak with other tongues, as the Spirit gave them utterance.

[20]

(1 Cor 13:8) Charity never fails: but whether there be prophecies, they shall fail; whether there be tongues, they shall cease; whether there be knowledge, it shall vanish away.

(2 Pt 1:20-21) Knowing this first, that no prophecy of the scripture is of any private interpretation. [21] For the prophecy came not in old time by the will of man: but holy men of God spoke as they were moved by the Holy Ghost.

(2 Sam 12:9) Wherefore hast thou despised the commandment of the LORD, to do evil in his sight? thou hast killed Uriah the Hittite with the sword, and hast taken his wife to be thy wife, and hast slain him with the sword of the children of Ammon.

(Gn 9:6) Whoso sheds man's blood, by man is his blood shed: for in the image of God hath He made man.

(Pr 13:24) He that spares his rod hates his son: but he that loves him chastens him betimes.

(Lk 16:18) Whosoever puts away his wife, and marries another, commits adultery: and whosoever marries her that is put away from her husband commits adultery.

(Titus 2:4-5) That they may teach the young women to be sober, to love their husbands, to love their children, [5] To be discreet, chaste, keepers at home, good, obedient to their own husbands, that the word of God be not blasphemed.

(1 Cor 7:34) The unmarried woman cares for the things of the Lord, that she may be holy both in body and in spirit: but she that is married cares for the things of the world, how she may please her husband.

[21]

(Eph 5:10) Proving what is acceptable unto the Lord.

(Phil 1:10) That you may approve things that are excellent; that ye may be sincere and without offence till the day of Christ.

(1 Jn 4:1) Beloved, believe not every spirit, but try the spirits whether they are of God: because many false prophets are gone out into the world.

(Jn 5:37) And the Father himself, which hath sent me, hath borne witness of me. You have neither heard his voice at any time, nor seen his shape.

[5:19-22]
[19][π] Quench not
the Spirit.
[20] Despise not
prophesyings.
[21] Prove all things;
hold fast that which
is good.
[22] Abstain from all
appearance of evil.

[19][π] Verses 19-22 clearly constitute a unit of information. The focus may be how Christians exercise discernment. The form of the unit begins with two parallel, negated lines (19-20). The pivotal line (21) brings together the two negative lines into a positive statement. The final two lines (21b-22) direct the results of the first three. It is a remarkable unit of expression (FIG 1). Although the translation of **quench not** and **despise not** could be *stop quenching* and *stop despising,* the context supports the accepted translation. **The Spirit** (τὸ πνεῦμα) is often related by the figure of fire (Ac 2:2-4). As such, believers are not to *douse* (σβέννυτε) the burning work of the Spirit in their lives. **For as many as are lead by the Spirit of God, these are the sons of God** (Ro 8:14). The urgings of the Holy Spirit must be obeyed. This concept seems to coordinate with the next line.

[20] The word **prophesyings** (προφητείας) can refer to the gift (I Cor 13:8) or written prophetic utterences (2 Pt 1:21). In this line, it appears to indicate all information revealed by God. To **despise** (ἐξουθενεῖτε) means *to count as nothing* or *give no weight to* (2 Sam 12:9). Sadly, many Christians selectively follow this course (e.g., Gn 9:6; Pr 13:24; Lk 16:18; Titus 2:4-5; 1 Cor 7:34b).

FIG 1

the Spirit, quench not
prophesies, despise not
BUT, all things, prove
the good, retain
from every form of evil, abstain

[21] Unfortunately, the adversative *but* (δὲ) that occurs in this verse is omitted in the KJV. Some manuscripts do not contain it. *But* **prove** (δοκιμάζετε) brings into a positive statement what the author desires to communicate. The product of **proving** is that which is approved. In this context it may be defined as biblically defensible behaviors (Eph 5:10; Phil 1:10). Living by the guidance of the Spirit (subjective, personal) and the revealed word (objective, normative to all believers) allows one to *evidence* (**prove**) what pleasing God consists of (1 Jn 4:1). The next two lines (21b, 22) begin the practical aspect. If **the good** be proven, then, *retain* (κατέχετε, **hold fast**) **the good**.

[22] There is a subtle change in the parallelism here. The good is naturally contrasted with the **evil**. Here, **from** *every form* (**all appearance**) **of evil** develops the contrast. The word **appearance** (εἴδους) usually refers to a bodily form (Jn 5:37). In this context, it draws from its classical use, denoting *kind* or *form.* Every type of vice, **abstain** (ἀπέχεσθε) from.

GREEK TEXT

[23][π] Αὐτὸς δὲ ὁ θεὸς τῆς εἰρήνης ἁγιάσαι ὑμᾶς ὁλοτελεῖς, καὶ ὁλόκληρον ὑμῶν τὸ πνεῦμα καὶ ἡ ψυχὴ καὶ τὸ σῶμα ἀμέμπτως ἐν τῇ παρουσίᾳ τοῦ κυρίου ἡμῶν Ἰησοῦ Χριστοῦ τηρηθείη. [24] πιστὸς ὁ καλῶν ὑμᾶς, ὃς καὶ ποιήσει.

[25][π] Ἀδελφοί, προσεύχεσθε [καὶ] περὶ ἡμῶν.

[26][π] Ἀσπάσασθε τοὺς ἀδελφοὺς πάντας ἐν φιλήματι ἁγίῳ.

REFERENCES

[24]
(Phil 2:13) For it is God which works in you both to will and to do of his good pleasure.
[25]
(Ro 12:12) Rejoicing in hope; patient in tribulation; continuing instant in prayer;

1 THESSALONIANS 5:23-26

Verses twenty-three and twenty-four contain the second and final prayer-wish of the letter. This wish finishes the section, asking God to work in their sanctification.

[5:23-25]
[23][π] And the very God of peace sanctify you wholly; and I pray God your whole spirit and soul and body be preserved blameless unto the coming of our Lord Jesus Christ.
[24] Faithful is he that calls you, who also will do it.
[25][π] Brethren, pray for us.
[26][π] Greet all the brethren with an holy kiss.

[23][π] **And** or *Now* (δὲ) again shows a division. Paul requests that **God** *himself* might completely **sanctify** the Thessalonians and *at* (**unto**) **the coming** (παρουσία) **of the Lord** they might be *kept* **blameless** (ἀμέμπτως). This verse has two parts: *Now, may the God of peace himself sanctify you [wholly and] completely, and may your spirit and soul and body be preserved blameless at the coming of our Lord Jesus Christ.* The requests: to become sanctified (*holy*), and to be kept sanctified at the **coming** (παρουσία) of the Lord Jesus Christ. [24] This verse is inseparable from verse twenty three. As God **calls us**, he bids us to sanctification (Phil 2:13), which work he *will* ultimately **do** and complete in our behalf.

The final four verses of the letter contain the closing in a postscript. In it are found a request for prayer, greetings, a charge and a grace wish.

[25][π] This postscript begins with **brethren** (Ἀδελφοί), a common marker for a new division. Paul requests prayer from his new converts. Apparently Paul believes that prayer is of equal weight and a shared responsibility among God's people. Although we don't pray for Paul's team today, mutual prayer remains a Christian's responsibility (Ro 12:12).
[26][π] What is a **holy kiss** (φιλήματι ἁγίῳ)? Have you ever received one? Certainly, sensuousness is absent in a holy kiss. In John Bunyan's day (England, 1628-1688), the church tried to revive this practice but found only the more "comely" members of the church were receiving "holy kisses". Thus, the practice was abandoned. It appears that this matter is culturally

TYPICAL
CLOSING
ELEMENTS

-health wish
-word of farewell
-travel plans
-prayer
-prayer request
-commendation of
fellow workers
-greetings (to and
from the group)

PERORATIO:
-final exhortation
-final issue

POSTSCRIPT:
-holy kiss
-autographed
greeting
-benediction
-doxology
-grace wish

GREEK TEXT

[26][π] Ἀσπάσασθε τοὺς ἀδελφοὺς πάντας ἐν φιλήματι ἁγίῳ.

[27][π] Ἐνορκίζω ὑμᾶς τὸν κύριον ἀναγνωσθῆναι τὴν ἐπιστολὴν πᾶσιν τοῖς ἀδελφοῖς.

[28][π] Ἡ χάρις τοῦ κυρίου ἡμῶν Ἰησοῦ Χριστοῦ μεθ' ὑμῶν.

REFERENCES

[28]

(Ro 16:22) I Tertius, who wrote this epistle, salute you in the Lord.

[5:26-28]
[26][π] Greet all the brethren with an holy kiss.
[27][π] I charge you by the Lord that this epistle be read unto all the holy brethren.
[28][π] The grace of our Lord Jesus Christ be with you. Amen.

tempered, appropriately coming in this personal section. Not withstanding, this command proposes a standard of individual, indiscriminate tender love.

[27][π] Paul now uses the first person (I) in a solemn **charge** (Ἐνορκίζω), citing **the Lord** in regard to the performance of the charge. Some believe that the first person indicates that Paul now ends the letter in his own writing, stepping in for an amanuensis (for example, Tertios, Ro 16:22; 2 Thes 3:17). The content of the charge: for **this epistle** (ἐπιστολὴν) **to be read** (ἀναγνωσθῆναι) **to all the brethren**.

[28][π] A benediction ends the letter. It is a brief but powerful statement of desire for the constant companionship of sustaining **grace** (2 Thes 3:18) among the brotherhood of the believers.

CHAPTER SIX

THE END IS NOT YET

SCHEMA OF
2 THESSALONIANS

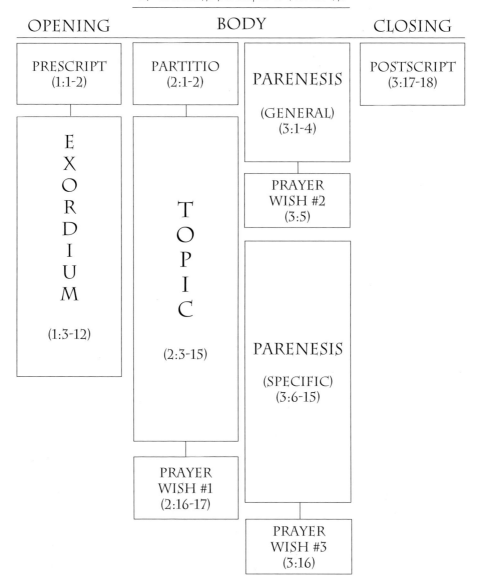

OPENING   BODY   CLOSING

PRESCRIPT
(1:1-2)

PARTITIO
(2:1-2)

PARENESIS

(GENERAL)
(3:1-4)

POSTSCRIPT
(3:17-18)

E
X
O
R
D
I
U
M

(1:3-12)

T
O
P
I
C

(2:3-15)

PRAYER
WISH #2
(3:5)

PARENESIS

(SPECIFIC)
(3:6-15)

PRAYER
WISH #1
(2:16-17)

PRAYER
WISH #3
(3:16)

GREEK TEXT

[1][π] Παῦλος καὶ Σιλουανὸς καὶ Τιμόθεος τῇ ἐκκλησίᾳ Θεσσαλονικέων ἐν θεῷ πατρὶ ἡμῶν καὶ κυρίῳ Ἰησοῦ Χριστῷ·

[2][π] χάρις ὑμῖν καὶ εἰρήνη ἀπὸ θεοῦ πατρὸς |omit| [UBS, ἡμῶν] καὶ κυρίου Ἰησοῦ Χριστοῦ.

[3][π] Εὐχαριστεῖν ὀφείλομεν τῷ θεῷ πάντοτε περὶ ὑμῶν, ἀδελφοί, καθὼς ἄξιόν ἐστιν, ὅτι ὑπεραυξάνει ἡ πίστις ὑμῶν καὶ πλεονάζει ἡ ἀγάπη ἑνὸς ἑκάστου πάντων ὑμῶν εἰς ἀλλήλους, [4] ὥστε αὐτοὺς ἡμᾶς ἐν ὑμῖν ἐγκαυχᾶσθαι ἐν ταῖς ἐκκλησίαις τοῦ θεοῦ ὑπὲρ τῆς ὑπομονῆς ὑμῶν καὶ πίστεως ἐν πᾶσιν τοῖς διωγμοῖς ὑμῶν καὶ ταῖς θλίψεσιν αἷς ἀνέχεσθε,

REFERENCES

[3]
(1 Thes 3:12) And the Lord make you to increase and abound in love one toward another, and toward all men, even as we do toward you:
(1 Thes 4:10) And indeed you do it toward all the brethren which are in all Macedonia: but we beseech you, brethren, that you increase more and more;
[4]
(1 Thes 1:6) And you became followers of us, and of the Lord, having received the word in much affliction, with joy of the Holy Ghost.
(Ac 14:19) And there came thither certain Jews from Antioch and Iconium, who persuaded the people, and having stoned Paul, drew him out of the city, supposing he had been dead.

Outlining a Pauline epistle by topical analysis
is like shoveling sand with a pitch fork.
It is the wrong tool for the job.

Chapter one serves as the opening to this letter. As is typical of the opening, it contains the prescript and exordium. Verses one and two are the prescript of this letter. In them we find the author, cosponsors, recipient, and a grace and peace wish.

[1:1-4]
[1][π] Paul, and Silvanus, and Timothy, unto the church of the Thessalonians in God our Father and the Lord Jesus Christ [2][π] Grace unto you, and peace, from God our Father and the Lord Jesus Christ. [3][π] We are bound to thank God always for you, brethren, as it is meet, because that your faith grows exceedingly, and the charity of every one of you all toward each other abounds; [4] So that we ourselves glory in you in the churches of God for your patience and faith in all your persecutions and tribulations that you endure:

[1][π] **Paul** is the author, **Silvanus and Timothy** are co-workers and cosponsors of the letter. Again **church** (τῇ ἐκκλησίᾳ) is singular, specifying that particular church that Paul's team planted as the addressee.

[2][π] This **grace/peace** wish duplicates that of the first letter (1:1b). May God be gracious to you and give you **peace**.

Verses three through twelve form the exordium of the letter. This section usually contains thanksgiving (3-10) and prayer (11-12). In form, the exordium often resembles a run-on sentence: one long sentence with many fused together clauses. Twelve of Paul's thirteen letters have exordiums (save Galatians).

[3][π] In this section, Paul seeks to gain a favorable acceptance for his letter while surfacing positive achievements and teaching. **Bound** means they *owe* or are *obligated* (ὀφείλομεν) **to thank God**.... Thanks is *worthy* (ἄξιόν) or **fitting because** their **faith** is *super-growing* (ὑπεραυξάνει) **and** *love* (Old English, **charity**) **abounds** or *multiplies* (πλεονάζει) on an individual basis (**every one of you**), just as Paul had prayed for (I Thes 3:12; 4:10).

[4] The result (**so that**, ὥστε) of such progress was Paul's *boasting* (**glory**, ἐγκαυχᾶσθαι) among the other **churches. For your** or *concerning your* **patience** (ὑπομονῆς) speaks of their endurance and perseverance although in *afflictions* (as before, 1 Thes 1:6) and **persecutions** (διωγμοῖς). This is the first and last reference to persecution in the Thessalonian epistles. After Paul is stoned in Lystra (Ac 14:19), his team spreads the news **that we must through much tribulation** (*affliction*) **enter into the kingdom of God** (v 22). Their **faith** was standing the test of opposition.

Pauline Recipients	
Individuals	Philemon, 1 & 2 Tim, Titus,
Church (sg)	1 & 2 Cor, 1 & 2 Thes
Churches	Ga
Saints (local)	Ro, Eph, Phil, Col

GREEK TEXT

[5] ἔνδειγμα τῆς δικαίας κρίσεως τοῦ θεοῦ, εἰς τὸ καταξιωθῆναι ὑμᾶς τῆς βασιλείας τοῦ θεοῦ, ὑπὲρ ἧς καὶ πάσχετε, [6] εἴπερ δίκαιον παρὰ θεῷ ἀνταποδοῦναι τοῖς θλίβουσιν ὑμᾶς θλῖψιν [7] καὶ ὑμῖν τοῖς θλιβομένοις ἄνεσιν μεθ' ἡμῶν ἐν τῇ ἀποκαλύψει τοῦ κυρίου Ἰησοῦ ἀπ' οὐρανοῦ μετ' ἀγγέλων δυνάμεως αὐτοῦ

REFERENCES

[5]
(1 Cor 2:4) And my speech and my preaching was not with enticing words of man's wisdom, but in demonstration of the Spirit and of power:
(1 Pet 4:12-19) Beloved, think it not strange concerning the fiery trial which is to try you, as though some strange thing happened unto you: [13] But rejoice, inasmuch as you are partakers of Christ's sufferings; that, when his glory shall be revealed, you may be glad also with exceeding joy. [14] If you be reproached for the name of Christ, happy are you; for the spirit of glory and of God rests upon you: on their part he is evil spoken of, but on your part he is glorified. [15] But let none of you suffer as a murderer, or as a thief, or as an evildoer, or as a busybody in other men's matters. [16] Yet if any man suffer as a Christian, let him not be ashamed; but let him glorify God on this behalf. [17] For the time is come that judgment must begin at the house of God: and if it first begin at us, what shall the end be of them that obey not the gospel of God? [18] And if the righteous scarcely be saved, where shall the ungodly and the sinner appear? [19] Wherefore let them that suffer according to the will of God commit the keeping of their souls to him in well doing, as unto a faithful Creator.
[6]
(Ro 12:19) Dearly beloved, avenge not yourselves, but rather give place unto wrath: for it is written, Vengeance is mine; I will repay, saith the Lord.
[7]
(2 Cor 8:13) For I mean not that other men be eased, and you burdened:
(Mt 25:31-34) When the Son of man shall come in his glory, and all the holy angels with him, then shall he sit upon the throne of his glory: [32] And before him shall be gathered all nations: and he shall separate them one from another, as a shepherd divides his sheep from the goats: [33] And he shall set the sheep on his right hand, but the goats on the left. [34] Then shall the King say unto them on his right hand, Come, blessed of my Father, inherit the kingdom prepared for you from the foundation of the world:

[5] Which is a manifest token of the righteous judgment of God, that you may be counted worthy of the kingdom of God, for which you also suffer: [6] Seeing it is a righteous thing with God to recompense tribulation to them that trouble you; [7] And to you who are troubled rest with us, when the Lord Jesus shall be revealed from heaven with his mighty angels,

[5] It has been noted that this verse is "difficult to follow". The first few words translate, *an evidence of the just judgment of God.* Is it speaking of their suffering or their conduct in suffering? **Manifest token** (ἔνδειγμα) can be translated as *evidence,* meaning what is demonstrated to be true (1 Cor 2:4). It may be taken this way; the troubles you are suffering are an evidence of the right decision of God for you to be considered worthy of the kingdom of God. In summary, their character commends God's decision of counting them worthy. **For** (*in behalf of*) **which you suffer** (πάσχετε) refers to the cause of their suffering: **the kingdom of God** (1 Pet 4:12-19). Had their course not been altered, their life would have the ease and simple difficulties as it had before. The Christian life is a struggle to row against the currents of society and be be treated unjustly.

Perseverance is the attitude that accepts trying circumstances without retarding progress. Bruce

[6] This verse begins with **seeing** (εἴπερ), which may be: *if, as is the fact, it is just.... Just* (δίκαιον) is in the sense of **righteous** in this context; what is just is the **recompense** (ἀνταποδοῦναι) or *retribution.* The term "conveys the thought of a full and due requital" (Morris)(Ro 12:19). The word play is significant, *to recompense affliction to those afflicting you, and to you being afflicted, rest.* Those who trouble believers align themselves against divine justice. It is far better to suffer for God than from God. Peter gives particular advice to those suffering: **But and if you suffer for righteousness' sake, happy are you: and be not afraid of their terror, neither be troubled; But sanctify the Lord God in your hearts: and be ready always to give an answer to every man... a reason of the hope that is in you....** (1 Pet 3:14-15).
[7] *But* may be better than **and** since a contrast now occurs. In speaking of financial equality, Paul uses the terms **rest** and **trouble: For I mean not that other men be eased, and you burdened** (2 Cor 8:13). When will this **rest** or *relief* (ἄνεσιν) occur? At the *revelation* (ἀποκαλύψει, *apocalypse*) *of the Lord Jesus.* There, grief is relieved; there, grief begins. At the second advent, at the end of the tribulation period, the enactment of justice begins (Mt 25:31-34). A just Judge will rule and rein in righteousness.

GREEK TEXT

[7] καὶ ὑμῖν τοῖς θλιβομένοις ἄνεσιν μεθ' ἡμῶν ἐν τῇ ἀποκαλύψει τοῦ κυρίου Ἰησοῦ ἀπ' οὐρανοῦ μετ' ἀγγέλων δυνάμεως αὐτοῦ [8] ἐν πυρὶ φλογός, διδόντος ἐκδίκησιν τοῖς μὴ εἰδόσιν θεὸν καὶ τοῖς μὴ ὑπακούουσιν τῷ εὐαγγελίῳ τοῦ κυρίου ἡμῶν Ἰησοῦ, [9] οἵτινες δίκην τίσουσιν ὄλεθρον αἰώνιον ἀπὸ προσώπου τοῦ κυρίου καὶ ἀπὸ τῆς δόξης τῆς ἰσχύος αὐτοῦ, [10] ὅταν ἔλθῃ ἐνδοξασθῆναι ἐν τοῖς ἁγίοις αὐτοῦ καὶ θαυμασθῆναι ἐν πᾶσιν τοῖς πιστεύσασιν, ὅτι ἐπιστεύθη τὸ μαρτύριον ἡμῶν ἐφ' ὑμᾶς, ἐν τῇ ἡμέρᾳ ἐκείνῃ.

REFERENCES

[8]

(Ex 3:2) And the angel of the LORD appeared unto him in a flame of fire out of the midst of a bush: and he looked, and, behold, the bush burned with fire, and the bush was not consumed.

(Rev 1:13 -14) And in the midst of the seven candlesticks one like unto the Son of man, clothed with a garment down to the foot, and girt about the paps with a golden girdle. [14] His head and his hairs were white like wool, as white as snow; and his eyes were as a flame of fire;

(Rev 19:11 -14) And I saw heaven opened, and behold a white horse; and he that sat upon him was called Faithful and True, and in righteousness he doth judge and make war. [12] His eyes were as a flame of fire, and on his head were many crowns; and he had a name written, that no man knew, but he himself. [13] And he was clothed with a vesture dipped in blood: and his name is called The Word of God. [14] And the armies which were in heaven followed him upon white horses, clothed in fine linen, white and clean.

(Ro 12:19) Dearly beloved, avenge not yourselves, but rather give place unto wrath: for it is written, Vengeance is mine; I will repay, saith the Lord.

(Mt 7:15)

[9]

(Lk 16:24 -26) And he cried and said, Father Abraham, have mercy on me, and send Lazarus, that he may dip the tip of his finger in water, and cool my tongue; for I am tormented in this flame. [25] But Abraham said, Son, remember that thou in thy lifetime received thy good things, and likewise Lazarus evil things: but now he is comforted, and thou art tormented. [26] And beside all this, between us and you there is a great gulf fixed: so that they which would pass from hence to you cannot; neither can they pass to us, that would come from thence.

[1:7-10]

[7] And to you who are troubled rest with us, when the Lord Jesus shall be revealed from heaven with his mighty angels, [8] In flaming fire taking vengeance on them that know not God, and that obey not the gospel of our Lord Jesus Christ: [9] Who shall be punished with everlasting destruction from the presence of the Lord, and from the glory of his power; [10] When he shall come to be glorified in his saints, and to be admired in all them that believe (because our testimony among you was believed) in that day.

When the Son of man shall come in his glory, and all the holy angels with him, then shall he sit upon the throne of his glory... and he shall separate them one from another... Then shall the King say unto them on his right hand, Come, blessed of my Father, inherit the kingdom prepared for you from the foundation of the world (Mt 25:31ff). It seems appropriate to speak of things settled at the Second Advent. There, eternal consequences will contrast temporal afflictions. [8] **Fire** (πυρὶ) is associated with the divine presence of God (Ex 3:2; Rev 1:13-14). Authors dispute whether this context moves this phrase toward a manifestation of majesty or physical fire (**flaming fire,** πυρὶ φλογός) as an instrument of judgment. Note Rev 19:11-14, **And I saw heaven opened, and behold a white horse; and he that sat upon him was called Faithful and True, and in righteousness he doth judge and make war. His eyes were as a flame of fire... And the armies which were in heaven followed him....** He will administer (lit., *giving*) **vengeance** or *vindication* (ἐκδίκησιν, Ro 12:19). "It is the inflicting of full justice on the criminal... nothing more, nothing less" (Findlay). The objects of vindication: *those who know not God and those who are obeying not the gospel of our Lord Jesus.* Knowing God and obeying the gospel are one in the same. The **gospel of our Lord Jesus Christ** (εὐαγγελίῳ) is the *good news* that salvation is by faith in the finished work of Jesus Christ. Favor with God cannot be earned; it must be granted.

Obedience to the gospel is not optional.

[9] **Who** (*those....* of v 8) or *which ones shall undergo justice: eternal ruin* (ὄλεθρον αἰώνιον). EBC takes it as "They will pay the penalty, everlasting destruction". Separation from **the Lord and from** *his glorious might* are part of the state of everlasting ruin (Lk 16:24-26). The punishment of unbelievers will never end and its severity will never be eased. [10] Verse ten contrasts verse nine. Some will be removed from his **glory;** others will take part in it. **Them that believe** (*the holy ones,* i.e., **saints**) will render glory and admiration to Him. Because the *witness* (**testimony**) of the team was accepted, they will take part in glorifying Him *at* **that day.** This is the hope that the believer awaits. Eventually and inevitably, the Christian wins.

GREEK TEXT

[11] εἰς ὃ καὶ προσευχόμεθα πάντοτε περὶ ὑμῶν, ἵνα ὑμᾶς ἀξιώσῃ τῆς κλήσεως ὁ θεὸς ἡμῶν καὶ πληρώσῃ πᾶσαν εὐδοκίαν ἀγαθωσύνης καὶ ἔργον πίστεως ἐν δυνάμει, [12] ὅπως ἐνδοξασθῇ τὸ ὄνομα τοῦ κυρίου ἡμῶν Ἰησοῦ ἐν ὑμῖν, καὶ ὑμεῖς ἐν αὐτῷ, κατὰ τὴν χάριν τοῦ θεοῦ ἡμῶν καὶ κυρίου Ἰησοῦ Χριστοῦ.

REFERENCES

[12]

(Jn 17:1 -5) Jesus spoke these words, lifted up His eyes to heaven, and said: "Father, the hour has come. Glorify Your Son, that Your Son also may glorify You, [2] as You have given Him authority over all flesh, that He should give eternal life to as many as You have given Him. [3] And this is eternal life, that they may know You, the only true God, and Jesus Christ whom You have sent. [4] I have glorified You on the earth. I have finished the work which You have given Me to do. [5] And now, O Father, glorify Me together with Yourself, with the glory which I had with You before the world was (NKJV).

[CHART]

(1 Cor 15:23) But every man in his own order: Christ the first fruits; afterward they that are Christ's at his coming.

(1 Cor 16:17) I am glad of the coming of Stephanas and Fortunatus and Achaicus: for that which was lacking on your part they have supplied.

(2 Cor 7:6-7) Nevertheless God, that comforts those that are cast down, comforted us by the coming of Titus; (7) And not by his coming only, but by the consolation wherewith he was comforted in you, when he told us your earnest desire, your mourning, your fervent mind toward me; so that I rejoiced the more.

(2 Cor 10:10) For his letters, say they, are weighty and powerful; but his bodily presence is weak, and his speech contemptible.

(Phil 1:26) That your rejoicing may be more abundant in Jesus Christ for me by my coming to you again.

(Phil 2:12) Wherefore, my beloved, as ye have always obeyed, not as in my presence only, but now much more in my absence, work out your own salvation with fear and trembling.

[1:11-12]
[11] Wherefore also we pray always for you, that our God would count you worthy of this calling, and fulfil all the good pleasure of his goodness, and the work of faith with power:
[12] That the name of our Lord Jesus Christ may be glorified in you, and you in him, according to the grace of our God and the Lord Jesus Christ.

[11] The second common division of the exordium, prayer, now begins. The term **wherefore** can be translated *unto which* or *concerning which* (εἰς ὅ), referring to the previous information (vv 3-10). Two aims constitute the emphasis of the team's (**we**) prayers for the Thessalonians. The NAB may summarize them well: *To this end, we always pray for you, [1] that our God may make you worthy of his calling and [2], that our God may powerfully bring to fulfillment every good purpose and every effort of faith.*

[12] The ultimate purpose of their efforts- **that the name of the Lord Jesus Christ may be glorified**.... This verse approaches the 'doxological purpose of man'. The question, What is the chief end of man?, has been catechized, answering - "to glorify God and enjoy him forever". The phrase **and you in him** is explained by Bicknell: "The relation between Christians and Christ is reciprocal. They too receive glory in virtue of what He has done for them" (Jn 17:1ff). This all works *on the basis of* (κατὰ, **according to**....) **the grace of God and the Lord Jesus Christ.**

Pauline uses of "coming" or "presence"
(*parousia*) speak of temporal visits.

	Whose Coming?
1 Cor 15:23	... those of Christ at his coming
1 Cor 16:17	Stephanas
2 Cor 7:6, 7	Titus
2 Cor 10:10	(Paul)
Phil 1:26	(Paul)
Phil 2:12	(Paul)
1 Thes 2:19	Lord Jesus Christ
3:13	Lord Jesus Christ
4:15	Lord Jesus Christ
5:23	Lord Jesus Christ
2 Thes 2:1	Lord Jesus Christ
2:8	Lord Jesus Christ
2:9	the Antichrist

HALL OF SHAME

When it comes to the date of the Day of the Lord, God has spoken with clarity: **no man knows the day nor the hour**. Many in the past and in the present take part in the work that troubled the Thessalonian believers. In so doing, they are alarmists, false prophets and do damage not only to those who trust in them but also the credibility of the scriptures. This is only a sample list.

"Judgment Day, May 21, 2011, THE BIBLE GUARANTEES IT!"

Harold Camping, Family Radio. Having listened to Mr. Camping for over twenty-five years, I can say with certainty that his hermeneutics are beyond a catastrophe. Mixing a fetish with numbers stemming from his civil engineering degree, with no Bible education whatsoever, has him painting a picture of the Bible wherein the sky is green, the grass is blue and the sun spins around the earth. Calling coincidences "proofs" and clear teaching, nonsense - as it pleases him, his views come together as a perfect storm of indefensible predictions that often change daily. It is no surprise then that he is a multiple offender. Consistently, in the minds of fools, numbers found in the Bible somehow abrogate the actual meaning of the words that convey truth.

September 15, 1994

Harold Camping. "In the Bible, we can learn how God plans to destroy the church...." (1994?, p. 169), "The AIDS plague dramatically warns that the end is near...." (1994?, p. 213), "To arrive at the two ends of time... God has to do something special with the numbers." (1994?, p. 404), "The Bible apparently assures us that the duration of the earth is to be 12,000 years" (1994?, p. 440), "1988.... was the beginning of the final tribulation" (1994?, p. 444), "390 days equals 3900 years" (1994?, p. 452), "Forty days equals 4000 years" (1994?, p. 453), "1290 brings us to the end of time" (1994?, p. 464), "... His second coming on the Day of Atonement, September 15, 1994, is entirely reasonable." (1994?, p. 521).

The year 1975....

"6,000 Years Completed in 1975... In what year, then, would the first 6,000 years of man's existence and also the first 6,000 years of God's rest day come to an end?
Awake! (October 8, 1966, pp. 19   -20. 'How Much Longer Will It Be?') Official JW publication.

"At Easter time in 1935, Jesus appeared to the young Sun Myung Moon as he was praying in the Korean mountains. Jesus asked him to complete the task of establishing God's kingdom on earth and bringing His peace to humankind."
Sun Myung Moon, (1920-present), founder and leader of the worldwide Unification Church.

"The Times of the Gentiles" will expire with the year 1914; and ... the advent of him whose right it is to take the dominion was due in 1874.... 1874 is the exact date of Our Lord's return.... Only twenty-four years of the harvest period remain...."
Charles Taze Russell (1852-1916), founder of the Jehovah Witnesses cult.

"In the year twenty-one hundred I think will be the end" (1904).
Mary Baker Eddy (1821-1910), founder of the Christian Science religion.

October 22, 1844 (The Great Disappointment)
"I believe that the second coming of Jesus Christ is near, even at the door, even within twenty-one years,—on or before 1843."
William Miller (1782-1849)(Millerism). Numbers, calendars, and readjusting the reading of times and events made this amateur student of the Bible a notable "Ism". Millerism is synonymous with fallacious predictions. Harold Camping's errors share a number of "coincidences" with Millerism.

"The scenes of earth's history are fast closing"
Ellen G. White (1827–1915), founder of the Seventh-day Adventist Church.

2 THESSALONIANS
TOPIC ANALYSIS 2:1-17

BODY

[1-2] Now, we are asking you, brethren, concerning the coming of our Lord Jesus Christ and our gathering unto him, for you to not be quickly rattled in your mind, neither to be alarmed, either by means of a spirit or a teaching or a letter– as from us, supposing that the day of the Lord has begun.

[3-4] Let no one trick you at all, because except the uprising might come first and the man of lawlessness might be revealed: the son of destruction, the one opposing and lifting himself above all being called God or that is venerated, so that he sits in the temple of God, presenting himself as God.

[5-12] You are remembering, are you not, that while yet being with you, I was telling you these things. And now you know that which is hindering for him to be revealed at his appointed time. For the mystery of lawlessness already is at work, only the one who is hindering now, until he might be out of the way, and then the Lawless One shall be revealed, whom the Lord shall smite with the blast of his mouth and shall destroy at the appearing of his coming, the coming of whom is in accord with the working of Satan, accompanied with all power and signs and deceiving wonders and with all deceitful deception among those being destroyed because they did not accept the love of the truth so that they might be saved. And because of this God sends to them a working of error so that they believe the lie, in order that all might be judged who did not believe the truth but rather delighted in unrighteousness.

[13-14] Now, we are obligated to thank God always concerning you, brethren beloved of the Lord, because God chose you as first fruits unto salvation by means of the sanctifying of the Spirit and faith in the truth, unto which he called you by means of our gospel, unto a glorious possession of our Lord Jesus Christ.

[15] Then therefore, brethren, take your stand and grasp the traditions which you were taught, whether through word, whether through our epistle.

[16-17] Now may our Lord Jesus Christ himself and God our Father, the one who loved us and gave us eternal comfort and good hope in grace, may he comfort your hearts and strengthen you in every good work and word.

Concerns:
Have we missed the rapture?
Has the Day of the Lord begun!?

Don't be fooled.
Two "first" things are missing.
-The Uprising and
-The Revealing of the Antichrist

You know what is hindering the Antichrist from being revealed. I told you.

God chose you for his possession.

Grab on to what you were taught.

Dear God:
Comfort them.
Strengthen them.

GREEK TEXT

[1][π] Ἐρωτῶμεν δὲ ὑμᾶς, ἀδελφοί, ὑπὲρ τῆς παρουσίας τοῦ κυρίου ἡμῶν Ἰησοῦ Χριστοῦ καὶ ἡμῶν ἐπισυναγωγῆς ἐπ' αὐτόν, [2] εἰς τὸ μὴ ταχέως σαλευθῆναι ὑμᾶς ἀπὸ τοῦ νοὸς μηδὲ θροεῖσθαι μήτε διὰ πνεύματος μήτε διὰ λόγου μήτε δι' ἐπιστολῆς ὡς δι' ἡμῶν, ὡς ὅτι ἐνέστηκεν ἡ ἡμέρα τοῦ κυρίου.

REFERENCES

[1]

(Ga 1:6) I marvel that you are so soon removed from him that called you into the grace of Christ unto another gospel:

(1 Cor 1:10) Now I beseech you, brethren, by the name of our Lord Jesus Christ, that you all speak the same thing, and that there be no divisions among you; but that you be perfectly joined together in the same mind and in the same judgment.

(Mt 23:37) O Jerusalem, Jerusalem, thou that killest the prophets, and stonest them which are sent unto thee, how often would I have gathered thy children together, even as a hen gathers her chickens under her wings, and you would not!

(Mt 24:31) And he shall send his angels with a great sound of a trumpet, and they shall gather together his elect from the four winds, from one end of heaven to the other.

(Lk 17:37) And they answered and said unto him, Where, Lord? And he said unto them, Wheresoever the body is, thither will the eagles be gathered together.

(1 Thes 4:13 -18) I would not have you to be ignorant, brethren, concerning them which are asleep, that ye sorrow not, even as others which have no hope. [14] For if we believe that Jesus died and rose again, even so them also which sleep in Jesus will God bring with him. [15] For this we say unto you by the word of the Lord, that we which are alive and remain unto the coming of the Lord shall not prevent them which are asleep. [16] For the Lord himself shall descend from heaven with a shout, with the voice of the archangel, and with the trump of God: and the dead in Christ shall rise first: [17] Then we which are alive and remain shall be caught up together with them in the clouds, to meet the Lord in the air: and so shall we ever be with the Lord. [18] Wherefore comfort one another with these words.

2 THESSALONIANS 2:1-2

*Chapter two contains the "big issue" or topic which
serves as the occasion for the letter. It is a key passage in
the study of eschatology (end times).
These verses (1-12) contain only three main clauses,
Now, we ask you, brethren,...
to be not soon shaken.... (v 1),
Let no man deceive you.... (v 3), and
You remember, do you not,...
I was telling you these things? (v 5).
Verses one and two are a partitio:
a division orienting and introducing the main section.*

[2:1-2]
[1][π] Now, we beseech you, brethren, by the coming of our Lord Jesus Christ, and by our gathering together unto him, [2] That you be not soon shaken in mind, or be troubled, neither by spirit, nor by word, nor by letter as from us, as that the day of Christ is at hand.

[1][π] The first sentence in the body of a letter usually exposes the writer's disposition toward the recipients and the issue at hand (Ga 1:6; 1 Cor 1:10). The formula, **Now, we** *ask* **you brethren** introduces a new section (δὲ... verb... ἀδελφοί). **Beseech** (Ἐρωτῶμεν) means to *ask* or *request*, showing a more positive avenue of instruction. What anchors this section is found in the next words, *concerning* (by, ὑπὲρ) **the coming** (*parousia*) **of our Lord Jesus Christ**... **and** [concerning] **our gathering together unto him**. The term **coming** (παρουσίας) speaks of a *visitation*. Inseparably linked grammatically to his coming is our **gathering unto him** (ἐπισυναγωγῆς, Mt 23:37, 24:31; Lk 17:37). This event, called the rapture comes from the word *caught* (Lat., *rapere*). It implies a sudden irresistible force, similar to Enoch being snatched away (**for God took him**, Gn 5:24). Note the perspectives: he comes and believers, including resurrected saints, are gathered in the clouds unto him (1 Thes 4:13-18).

[2] Verse two completes the sentence beginning in verse one, **we beseech you... that you be not soon shaken**.... The stated purpose for this passage is the removal of fear regarding the rapture (v 1)(which would be past if the Day of the Lord has begun) and the Day of the Lord (v 2f). This verse has many subtleties, *for you to not be shaken from your wits; not even to be in a state of alarm, whether by means of a spirit, whether by means of some declaration, whether by means of an epistle- as from us, supposing that the Day of the Lord has commenced.*

This section [2:1-12] contains truths found
nowhere else in the Bible. BKC

GREEK TEXT

[1][π] Ἐρωτῶμεν δὲ ὑμᾶς, ἀδελφοί, ὑπὲρ τῆς παρουσίας τοῦ κυρίου ἡμῶν Ἰησοῦ Χριστοῦ καὶ ἡμῶν ἐπισυναγωγῆς ἐπ' αὐτόν, [2] εἰς τὸ μὴ ταχέως σαλευθῆναι ὑμᾶς ἀπὸ τοῦ νοὸς μηδὲ θροεῖσθαι μήτε διὰ πνεύματος μήτε διὰ λόγου μήτε δι' ἐπιστολῆς ὡς δι' ἡμῶν, ὡς ὅτι ἐνέστηκεν ἡ ἡμέρα τοῦ κυρίου.

REFERENCES

[2]

(Lk 6:48-49) He is like a man which built an house, and dug deep, and laid the foundation on a rock: and when the flood arose, the stream beat vehemently upon that house, and could not shake it: for it was founded upon a rock. [49] But he that hears, and doeth not, is like a man that without a foundation built an house upon the earth; against which the stream did beat vehemently, and immediately it fell; and the ruin of that house was great.

(Eph 1:13) In whom you also trusted, after that you heard the word of truth, the gospel of your salvation: in whom also after that you believed, you were sealed with that holy Spirit of promise,

(2 Cor 1:18) But as God is true, our word toward you was not yea and nay.

[2:2]
[2] That you be not soon shaken in mind, or be troubled, neither by spirit, nor by word, nor by letter as from us, as that the day of Christ is at hand.

In picturesque language, Paul tells them to **be not shaken** (σαλευθῆναι) like the house built on the sand (Lk 6:48-49). **Soon** (ταχέως) is added, prohibiting the undo haste often occurring with fear. The phrase **in mind**, literally is *from your mind*. The first appeal is for a restoration of calm thinking ("mental equilibrium"). The second clause coordinates with the first. To not **be troubled** (θροεῖσθαι) is the same word used in Mt 24:6, **And you shall hear of wars and rumors of wars, see that you be not troubled: for all these things must come to pass, but the end is not yet**. The next three phrases speak of the avenues by which trouble can come and may have actually come to the Thessalonians. The first is a **spirit** (πνεύματος). This is not the Holy Spirit. John warned, **try the spirits whether they are of God** (1 Jn 4:1). Seldom is error presented without assurances of Spirit leading. The second is a **word** (λόγου, Eph 1:13; 2 Cor 1:18), meaning any message or treatise communicated to them. No writing or rhetoric should unnerve their faith. Paper never refuses ink. The third is a **letter** (*epistle*, ἐπιστολῆς) - **as from us**. The question naturally follows; did they receive a pseudo-Pauline letter? If they did not, why add such a specific statement? Morris notes, "...he writes in general terms, and we are probably justified in inferring that he was not quite sure of exactly what had happened". The sum of these three drives the point- let nothing alarm you regarding the issue at hand. **As** (ὡς) may be taken as *supposing* or dynamically, *as if*. The final clause contains the locus of the problem. The content and source of alarm was the false view **that the day of the Lord is at hand**: literally, *the day of the Lord has begun and is occurring now* (ἐνέστηκεν). "The erroneous message which all these voices echoed was that the day of the Lord had arrived; the Thessalonians were in it" (BKC). The phrase **the day of the Lord** does not refer to a twenty-four hour period, but rather a "program of events" (Pentecost) beginning at the rapture and continuing through to the millennial reign of Christ. The first century church is not unique in undergoing alarm from those teaching erroneous errors regarding prophesy. It somehow seems a natural match for cults and the 'self-taught' to manufacture delusive error on this topic. Typically, present world difficulties and events are used as "proofs" for their error.

> ## The end
> ## is not yet.

GREEK TEXT

[3][π] μή τις ὑμᾶς ἐξαπατήσῃ κατὰ μηδένα τρόπον· ὅτι ἐὰν μὴ ἔλθῃ ἡ ἀποστασία πρῶτον καὶ ἀποκαλυφθῇ ὁ ἄνθρωπος τῆς ἀνομίας, ὁ υἱὸς τῆς ἀπωλείας,

REFERENCES

[3]

(2 Cor 11:3) But I fear, lest by any means, as the serpent beguiled Eve through his subtilty, so your minds should be corrupted from the simplicity that is in Christ.

(1 Tim 2:14) And Adam was not deceived, but the woman being deceived was in the transgression.

(Ro 16:18) For they that are such serve not our Lord Jesus Christ, but their own belly; and by good words and fair speeches deceive the hearts of the simple.

(Ac 21:21) And they are informed of thee, that you teach all the Jews which are among the Gentiles to *forsake* Moses, saying that they ought not to circumcise their children, neither to walk after the customs.

(Rev 6ff) And I saw when the Lamb opened one of the seals, and I heard, as it were the noise of thunder, one of the four beasts saying, Come and see. [2] And I saw, and behold a white horse: and he that sat on him had a bow; and a crown was given unto him: and he went forth conquering, and to conquer. [3] And when he had opened the second seal, I heard the second beast say, Come and see. [4] And there went out another horse that was red: and power was given to him that sat thereon to take peace from the earth, and that they should kill one another: and there was given unto him a great sword. [5] And when he had opened the third seal, I heard the third beast say, Come and see. And I beheld, and lo a black horse; and he that sat on him had a pair of balances in his hand. [6] And I heard a voice in the midst of the four beasts say, A measure of wheat for a penny, and three measures of barley for a penny; and see thou hurt not the oil and the wine. [7] And when he had opened the fourth seal, I heard the voice of the fourth beast say, Come and see. [8] And I looked, and behold a pale horse: and his name that sat on him was Death, and Hell followed with him. And power was given unto them over the fourth part of the earth, to kill with sword, and with hunger, and with death, and with the beasts of the earth. [9] And when he had opened the fifth seal, I saw under the altar the souls of them that were slain for the word of God, and for the testimony which they held:

*Verses three through fifteen form
the topic section of this epistle.
It is termed a probatio, since the topic is treated
with explanation, argumentation, and exhortations.*

[2:3]
[3][π] Let no man deceive you by any means: for that day shall not come, except there come a falling away first, and that man of sin be revealed, the son of perdition;

[3][π] Paul begins with a directive; **Let no man deceive you.** **Deceive** (ἐξαπατήσῃ) is not the more common word for leading astray. Here, Paul chooses the term he uses twice of Eve (2 Cor 11:3; 1 Tim 2:14). It means to *trick* or *beguile* or *fool,* as Eve was deceived (Ro 16:18). **By any means** (κατὰ μηδένα τρόπον) indicates nothing is to be yielded. Didactic supports now reinforce Paul's proposition. **For** (ὅτι) or *because, except the apostasy might come first and the man of lawlessness might be revealed....* Paul sets forth two 'first things', demonstrating that they could not possibly be in the beginning events of the Day of the Lord. The first event they would recognize is called *ha apostasia* (Gk.), **the falling away** (ἀποστασία, Ac 21:21†). FIG 1 illustrates some contemporary understandings of this term. This chart coincides with FIG 2, which illustrates the timing of the possible meanings. The writer sees the term denoting an *uprising* (Rev 6ff). It seems that to prove Paul's point, his citation of events must fall within the Day of the Lord and be distinguishable from normal, even somewhat abnormal events. Thus, immanency (He can come at any time) is preserved in this view.

FIG 1

2 Thessalonians 2:3, "... a falling away first...."			
	Possible Meaning	Timing	Comments
A, B	"Apostasy" moral decline	Before the rapture or immediately following	Before: questions immanency. After: apostasy from what? by whom?
B	"Insurrection" or "Uprising"	Immediately after the rapture	This view coincides well with Revelation and this context
C	"Departure"	Departure is the rapture	Very weak lexical evidence and context

FIG 2

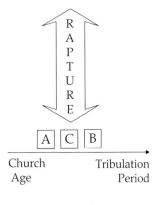

Church Age ——————————— Tribulation Period

GREEK TEXT

[3][π] μή τις ὑμᾶς ἐξαπατήσῃ κατὰ μηδένα τρόπον· ὅτι ἐὰν μὴ ἔλθῃ ἡ ἀποστασία πρῶτον καὶ ἀποκαλυφθῇ ὁ ἄνθρωπος τῆς ἀνομίας, ὁ υἱὸς τῆς ἀπωλείας, [4] ὁ ἀντικείμενος καὶ ὑπεραιρόμενος ἐπὶ πάντα λεγόμενον θεὸν ἢ σέβασμα, ὥστε αὐτὸν εἰς τὸν ναὸν τοῦ θεοῦ καθίσαι, ἀποδεικνύντα ἑαυτὸν ὅτι ἔστιν θεός. [5] Οὐ μνημονεύετε ὅτι ἔτι ὢν πρὸς ὑμᾶς ταῦτα ἔλεγον ὑμῖν;

REFERENCES

[3]

(Rev 6:1 -2) And I saw when the Lamb opened one of the seals, and I heard, as it were the noise of thunder, one of the four beasts saying, Come and see. [2] And I saw, and behold a white horse: and he that sat on him had a bow; and a crown was given unto him: and he went forth conquering, and to conquer.

(Jn 17:12) While I was with them in the world, I kept them in thy name: those that you gave me I have kept, and none of them is lost, but the son of perdition; that the scripture might be fulfilled.

[4]

(Mt 24:15 -16) When you therefore shall see the abomination of desolation, spoken of by Daniel the prophet, stand in the holy place, (whoso reads, let him understand:) [16] Then let them which be in Judea flee into the mountains:

(Rev 7:23-27) Thus he said, The fourth beast shall be the fourth kingdom upon earth, which shall be diverse from all kingdoms, and shall devour the whole earth, and shall tread it down, and break it in pieces. [24] And the ten horns out of this kingdom are ten kings that shall arise: and another shall rise after them; and he shall be diverse from the first, and he shall subdue three kings. [25] And he shall speak great words against the most High, and shall wear out the saints of the most High, and think to change times and laws: and they shall be given into his hand until a time and times and the dividing of time. [26] But the judgment shall sit, and they shall take away his dominion, to consume and to destroy it unto the end. [27] And the kingdom and dominion, and the greatness of the kingdom under the whole heaven, shall be given to the people of the saints of the most High, whose kingdom is an everlasting kingdom, and all dominions shall serve and obey him.

(Rev 11:1 -2) And there was given me a reed like unto a rod: and the angel stood, saying, Rise, and measure the temple of God, and the altar, and them that worship therein. [2] But the court which is without the temple leave out, and measure it not; for it is given unto the Gentiles: and the holy city shall they tread under foot forty and two months.

[2:3-5]
[3][π] Let no man deceive you by any means: for that day shall not come, except there come a falling away first, and that man of sin be revealed, the son of perdition; **[4]** Who opposes and exalts himself above all that is called God, or that is worshipped; so that he as God sits in the temple of God, showing himself that he is God. **[5][π]** Remember not, that, when I was yet with you, I told you these things?

The second proof is the revealing of the Antichrist. His revealing is stated as a divine passive (ἀποκαλυφθῇ) - he *shall* be revealed, i.e., God shall reveal him. No one will I.D. him until after the Day of the Lord begins. Bruce calls him "The leader of the great rebellion". Many see him as the white horseman of Rev 6:1-2, which is the first earthly scene in Revelation (after the first three chapters). He is called a **man** (ὁ ἄνθρωπος, *anthropos*) characterized by **sin** or *law-lessness* (ἀνομίας). He is "the doomed One" in that his inheritance is *destruction* (**perdition**, ἀπωλείας); he is its **son** (Judas, Jn 17:12). Destruction conceived him. History can be used to illustrate the logic of this passage. For example, what person and event proves that we are not living in November of 1863? The answer would be Abraham Lincoln and the Civil War. What person and event proved to the Thessalonians they were not in the Day of the Lord? The absence of the Uprising and the Revealing of the Antichrist. An individual and an event have not come upon the scene.

[4] He is the one **who opposes** (*remaining against*, ἀντικείμενος) **all that is called God** and who **exalts** (*lifting above*, ὑπεραιρόμενος) **himself above all that is called God**. All that is *venerated* (**worshipped**, σέβασμα) or considered worthy of worship he will oppose and lift himself above. The result (indicated by **so that**, ὥστε), suggesting sequence and time, is that he will present himself as God and reside in the rebuilt **temple** in Jerusalem in the holy place (ναὸν)(Mt 24:15-16; Rev 7:23-27, Rev 11:1-2).

At the rapture, history ceases to repeat itself. All familiar contexts pass away.

[5] This is the third main clause in this section (3-12). In what appears to be a simple verse, we find many nuances of meaning. First, in negated (**not**) questions, the writer often exposes his disposition toward the recipient by the use of one of two different negatives (οὐ and μη). Here, Paul displays a positive posture in asking, *you are remembering, are you not...?*, as opposed to *you don't remember, do you..!?* **I told you** is better *these things I was telling you?* Ignorance can seldom be cited as a valid excuse. A careful, appropriate disposition is found in these lines, teaching new converts who may be in a serious state of alarm.

GREEK TEXT

[6] καὶ νῦν τὸ κατέχον οἴδατε, εἰς τὸ ἀποκαλυφθῆναι αὐτὸν ἐν τῷ ἑαυτοῦ καιρῷ.

REFERENCES

[6]

(Jn 16:7 -11) Nevertheless I tell you the truth; It is expedient for you that I go away: for if I go not away, the Comforter will not come unto you; but if I depart, I will send him unto you. [8] And when he is come, he will reprove the world of sin, and of righteousness, and of judgment: [9] Of sin, because they believe not on me; [10] Of righteousness, because I go to my Father, and you see me no more; [11] Of judgment, because the prince of this world is judged.

[2:6]
[6] And now you know what restrains that he might be revealed in his time.

[6] You already know what is holding this wicked one back until it is time for him to come. [CEV]

[6] **And** (καὶ) could be *even* here. One of the great debates of 2 Thessalonians is found in verses six and seven. The terms **what restrains** (impersonal) and **he who hindereth** (v 7, personal) denote the same entity. What or who do they refer to? Both are from the same Greek word (κατέχω). Saint Augustine in *The City of God*, stated, "I admit that the meaning of this completely escapes me". Morris notes, "Since they knew what he was writing about, he had no need to be specific. He has accordingly left his allusion so general that commentators through the centuries have been baffled as to exactly what he did mean...." Bruce says that "they knew because they had been told and later readers are at a disadvantage compared with them, and have to guess". Suggestions for a referent include the Roman Empire, the Holy Spirit (a common view based on such passages as Jn 16:7-11), and the Church Universal. The Roman Empire view has long passed since that empire has long passed. The Spirit view is in question due to the phrase taken out of the way (v 7). The Church Universal, removed at the rapture, fits well with the scheme of last times. Its difficulty comes when trying to resolve the masculine and neuter terms with *ekklasia* (church), which is feminine in gender. To many the temptation to guess seems irresistible, "What was the restraining force which was still keeping the Lawless One under control? No one can answer that question with certainty. Most likely Paul meant the Roman Empire" (Barclay). In any case, the Thessalonians knew and Paul reminds them that something presides that could not, if the Day of the Lord has begun. The restraint must be removed *so that he* (the Antichrist) *might be revealed at his own appointed* **time** (καιρῷ, 1 Thes 5:1). Again the passive of **revealed** is used (ἀποκαλυφθῆναι, 2:3). These events are not the result of progressing history, but are that of divine intervention.

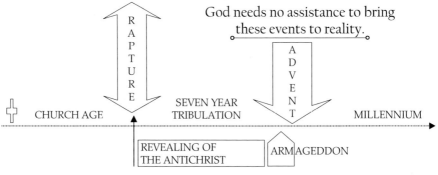

God needs no assistance to bring these events to reality.

RAPTURE

ADVENT

CHURCH AGE — SEVEN YEAR TRIBULATION — MILLENNIUM

REVEALING OF THE ANTICHRIST

ARMAGEDDON

GREEK TEXT

[7] τὸ γὰρ μυστήριον ἤδη ἐνεργεῖται τῆς ἀνομίας: μόνον ὁ κατέχων ἄρτι ἕως ἐκ μέσου γένηται. [8] καὶ τότε ἀποκαλυφθήσεται ὁ ἄνομος, ὃν ὁ κύριος [Ἰησοῦς] ἀνελεῖ τῷ πνεύματι τοῦ στόματος αὐτοῦ καὶ καταργήσει τῇ ἐπιφανείᾳ τῆς παρουσίας αὐτοῦ,

REFERENCES

[7]
(1 Jn 3:4) Whosoever commits sin transgresses also the law: for sin is the transgression of the law.
[8]
(Rev 19:11 -21) And I saw heaven opened, and behold a white horse; and he that sat upon him was called Faithful and True, and in righteousness he doth judge and make war. [12] His eyes were as a flame of fire, and on his head were many crowns; and he had a name written, that no man knew, but he himself. [13] And he was clothed with a vesture dipped in blood: and his name is called The Word of God. [14] And the armies which were in heaven followed him upon white horses, clothed in fine linen, white and clean. [15] And out of his mouth goes a sharp sword, that with it he should smite the nations: and he shall rule them with a rod of iron: and he treads the winepress of the fierceness and wrath of Almighty God. [16] And he hath on his vesture and on his thigh a name written, KING OF KINGS, AND LORD OF LORDS. [17] And I saw an angel standing in the sun; and he cried with a loud voice, saying to all the fowls that fly in the midst of heaven, Come and gather yourselves together unto the supper of the great God; [18] That ye may eat the flesh of kings, and the flesh of captains, and the flesh of mighty men, and the flesh of horses, and of them that sit on them, and the flesh of all men, both free and bond, both small and great. [19] And I saw the beast, and the kings of the earth, and their armies, gathered together to make war against him that sat on the horse, and against his army. [20] And the beast was taken, and with him the false prophet that wrought miracles before him, with which he deceived them that had received the mark of the beast, and them that worshipped his image. These both were cast alive into a lake of fire burning with brimstone. [21] And the remnant were slain with the sword of him that sat upon the horse, which sword proceeded out of his mouth: and all the fowls were filled with their flesh.
(Titus 2:13) Looking for that blessed hope, and the glorious appearing of the great God and our Savior Jesus Christ;

[2:7-8]
[7] For the mystery of lawlessness is already at work; only he who now restrains will do so until he is taken out of the way.
[NKJV]
[8] And then shall that Wicked be revealed, whom the Lord shall consume with the spirit of his mouth, and shall destroy with the brightness of his coming:

[7] **For** (γὰρ) is commonly used in citing a reason or setting forth argumentation. Paul admits that there is a working of *lawlessness* (**iniquity**, ἀνομίας, 1 Jn 3:4) presently occurring. It is called a **mystery** (μυστήριον) because it "works beneath the surface" (Bruce) yet culminates and unfolds in the Antichrist. The admission of this fact might be a part of the reconstruction of what type of information was being used to unsettle the Thessalonians. It is quite possible that present events and difficulties were being considered as fulfillment events. Such avenues of deception are common in our culture. On the heels of his admission: **only** *the one who is hindering now....* The timing sequences of vv 7-8 is noteworthy: **already... now... will continue to... until... and then shall be... shall... shall....** The term **hinders** (ὁ κατέχων, *restrains*, NKJV), from the same word **restrains** (v 6), is in the present tense, denoting a continual hindering like a lid holding down the pressure of a boiling pot. Some teach that there could be a "gap" as large as a thousand years between the rapture and the revealing of the Antichrist. This would allow him to come to power. The gap view violates the meaning of the words in this text, as well as, the characterization of divine jurisdiction over the events of the Day of the Lord. The exit of the restrainer (**he**) "from the scene" (**out of the way**)(Zerwick) immediately ushers in the revealing of the Antichrist.

[8] When will **the wicked** or *lawless* **one** (ὁ ἄνομος) **be revealed**? Immediately (**now... until... and then**) following the removal (**out of the way**, v 7) of the restrainer. Again, many view the referent here as the Comforter or Holy Spirit who is said to **reprove the world of sin, and of righteousness, and of judgment** (Jn 16:7-8). This is the third time **revealed** appears, being used of the Antichrist. Note how it is passive all three times, indicating that God will cause the revealing of this man (divine passive). Another evidence that the Day of the Lord has not begun is that the restrainer is present, and the Antichrist unrevealed. **Whom** (ὃν) begins a long digression on the Antichrist. He it is that **the Lord shall** *kill* or *destroy* (**consume**, ἀνελεῖ). This will transpire at the Revelation or Second Advent (Rev 19:11ff). The word **spirit** may better be *breath* (πνεύματι); the word has several options. The context (**of his mouth**) helps to determine which definition is best. He shall also **destroy** him **with the brightness** (ἐπιφανείᾳ) **of his coming** (1:7, 8; Titus 2:13).

GREEK TEXT

[9] οὗ ἐστιν ἡ παρουσία κατ᾽ ἐνέργειαν τοῦ Σατανᾶ ἐν πάσῃ δυνάμει καὶ σημείοις καὶ τέρασιν ψεύδους [10] καὶ ἐν πάσῃ ἀπάτῃ ἀδικίας τοῖς ἀπολλυμένοις, ἀνθ᾽ ὧν τὴν ἀγάπην τῆς ἀληθείας οὐκ ἐδέξαντο εἰς τὸ σωθῆναι αὐτούς. [11] καὶ διὰ τοῦτο πέμπει αὐτοῖς ὁ θεὸς ἐνέργειαν πλάνης εἰς τὸ πιστεῦσαι αὐτοὺς τῷ ψεύδει, [12] ἵνα κριθῶσιν πάντες οἱ μὴ πιστεύσαντες τῇ ἀληθείᾳ ἀλλὰ εὐδοκήσαντες τῇ ἀδικίᾳ.

REFERENCES

[9]
(Rev 13:14) And deceives them that dwell on the earth by the means of those miracles which he had power to do in the sight of the beast; saying to them that dwell on the earth, that they should make an image to the beast, which had the wound by a sword, and did live.
(Rev 19:20) And the beast was taken, and with him the false prophet that wrought miracles before him, with which he deceived them that had received the mark of the beast, and them that worshipped his image. These both were cast alive into a lake of fire burning with brimstone.
[11]
(Rev 6:15-16) And the kings of the earth, and the great men, and the rich men, and the chief captains, and the mighty men, and every bondman, and every free man, hid themselves in the dens and in the rocks of the mountains; [16] And said to the mountains and rocks, Fall on us, and hide us from the face of him that sits on the throne, and from the wrath of the Lamb:
(Isa 29:10-13) For the LORD hath poured out upon you the spirit of deep sleep, and hath closed your eyes: the prophets and your rulers, the seers hath he covered. [11] And the vision of all is become unto you as the words of a book that is sealed, which men deliver to one that is learned, saying, Read this, I pray thee: and he saith, I cannot; for it is sealed: [12] And the book is delivered to him that is not learned, saying, Read this, I pray thee: and he saith, I am not learned. [13] Wherefore the Lord said, Forasmuch as this people draw near me with their mouth, and with their lips do honor me, but have removed their heart far from me, and their fear toward me is taught by the precept of men:
(Ex 7:14, 22) And the LORD said unto Moses, Pharaoh's heart is hardened....
(Ex 11:10) ... and the LORD hardened Pharaoh's heart, so that he would not let the children of Israel go out of his land.
[12]
(Rev 7) And after these things I saw four angels standing on the four corners of the earth, holding the four winds of the earth, that the wind should not blow on the earth, nor on the sea, nor on any tree. [2] And I saw another angel ascending from the east, having the seal of the living God: and he cried with a loud voice to the four angels, to whom it was given to hurt the earth and the sea, [3] Saying, Hurt not the earth, neither the sea, nor the trees, till we have sealed the servants of our God in their foreheads.... [14] These are they which came out of great tribulation, and have washed their robes, and made them white in the blood of the Lamb....
(Rev 9:20-21) And the rest of the men which were not killed by these plagues yet repented not of the works of their hands, that they should not worship devils, and idols of gold, and silver, and brass, and stone, and of wood: which neither can see, nor hear, nor walk: [21] Neither repented they of their murders, nor of their sorceries, nor of their fornication, nor of their thefts.

[2:9-12]
[9] Even him, whose
coming is after the
working of Satan with
all power and signs
and lying wonders,
[10] And with all
deceivableness of
unrighteousness in
them that perish;
because they received
not the love of the
truth, that they might
be saved.
[11] And for this cause
God shall send them
strong delusion, that
they should believe a
lie:
[12] That they all
might be damned who
believed not the truth,
but had pleasure in
unrighteousness.

[9] This verse continues to speak of **him whose coming** (*parousia*) *is in accord with* **the working** (ἐνέργειαν, ...*energy*) **of Satan**. He, the Antichrist, works with satanic, supernatural **power** (δυνάμει), exhibiting miraculous **signs** (σημείοις)(Rev 13:14, 19:20), and *deceptive* (**lying**) wonders (τέρασιν ψεύδους). His **coming** is also *with every deception of unrighteousness among "those on the road to" destruction.*
[10] The wicked are in this situation because **they received not the love of the truth** *so that* **they might be saved**. Here, the past tense (**they received not**) takes a viewpoint from within the Tribulation. As Satan works through the Antichrist, men become deceived in spite of the option of embracing the truth. In these verses there is a progression of events showing that restraint is still present and evil is somewhat in check.
[11] *Consequently* (**and for this cause**), as a result of rejecting the truth, **God** *sends* (πέμπει, dramatic present) *a working of error* or **strong delusion** *so that they believe the lie.* Zerwick depicts it as "a force of deceiving power". Many ridiculous and self serving suggestions have been offered as to the content of **the lie**. For instance, that the lie is the teaching of evolution. The global, cataclysmic events of the tribulation seem to erase any notion of evolution, even among the wicked (Rev 6:15-16). **The lie** is not "lies" but singular (τῷ ψεύδει), likely referring to the Antichrist's assertion of himself as God (v 4). God's actions in this verse have been termed "judicial blinding". **For the LORD hath poured out upon you the spirit of deep sleep, and hath closed your eyes....** (Isa 29:10ff). No better example of this sealing of decision can be found than Pharaoh. After Pharaohs' many rejec-

All that appears miraculous
is not necessarily of God.

tions (Ex 7:14, 22, 8:32, 9:35), God hardens and seals the decision and fate of the Egyptian king (Ex 11:10).
[12] The purpose of God's working, to hold men to their chosen position of unbelief, is *so that all who believed not in the truth but rather took pleasure in unrighteousness might be judged* (**damned**, κριθῶσιν). Although some teach that unbelievers are sealed in unbelief at the rapture, this text indicates both choice (**believed not**) within the tribulation period and pleasure in that choice. **And the rest of the men which were not killed by these plagues yet repented not of the works of their hands... Neither repented they of their murders, sorceries, fornication, or thefts** (Rev 9:20-21, 7:1ff).

GREEK TEXT

[13][π] Ἡμεῖς δὲ ὀφείλομεν εὐχαριστεῖν τῷ θεῷ πάντοτε περὶ ὑμῶν, ἀδελφοὶ ἠγαπημένοι ὑπὸ κυρίου, ὅτι εἵλατο ὑμᾶς ὁ θεὸς Ιἀπ᾽ ἀρχῆςΙ [UBS, ἀπαρχὴν] εἰς σωτηρίαν ἐν ἁγιασμῷ πνεύματος καὶ πίστει ἀληθείας, [14] εἰς ὃ Ιomitι [UBS, καὶ] ἐκάλεσεν ὑμᾶς διὰ τοῦ εὐαγγελίου ἡμῶν, εἰς περιποίησιν δόξης τοῦ κυρίου ἡμῶν Ἰησοῦ Χριστοῦ.

[15][π] ἄρα οὖν, ἀδελφοί, στήκετε, καὶ κρατεῖτε τὰς παραδόσεις ἃς ἐδιδάχθητε εἴτε διὰ λόγου εἴτε δι᾽ ἐπιστολῆς ἡμῶν.

REFERENCES

[13]

(Ro 16:5) Likewise greet the church that is in their house. Salute my well-beloved Epaenetus who is the first fruits of Achaia unto Christ.

(1 Cor 16:15) I beseech you, brethren, (you know the house of Stephanas, that it is the first fruits of Achaia, and that they have addicted themselves to the ministry of the saints,)

(Titus 3:5) Not by works of righteousness which we have done, but according to his mercy he saved us, by the washing of regeneration, and renewing of the Holy Ghost;

(Eph 1:13) In whom you also trusted, after you heard the word of truth, the gospel of your salvation: in whom also after that you believed, you were sealed with that holy Spirit of promise,

[14]

(Ga 1:6-7a) I marvel that you are so soon removed from him that called you into the grace of Christ unto another gospel: [7] Which is not another....

(Eph 1:14) Which is the earnest of our inheritance until the redemption of the purchased possession, unto the praise of his glory.

[15]

(Phil 1:27) Only let your conversation be as it becomes the gospel of Christ: that whether I come and see you, or else be absent, I may hear of your affairs, that you stand fast in one spirit, with one mind striving together for the faith of the gospel;

(Ro 14:4) Who art thou that judges another man's servant? to his own master he stands or falls. Yea, he shall be held up: for God is able to make him stand.

(1 Cor 16:13) Watch, stand in the faith; be men, be strong; (Young's)

2 THESSALONIANS 2:13-15

[2:13-15]
[13][π] But we are bound to give thanks alway to God for you, brethren beloved of the Lord, because God hath from the beginning chosen you to salvation through sanctification of the Spirit and belief of the truth:
[14] Whereunto he called you by our gospel, to the obtaining of the glory of our Lord Jesus Christ.
[15][π] Therefore, brethren, stand fast, and hold the traditions which you have been taught, whether by word, or our epistle.

[13][π] Verses thirteen through fifteen complete the topic section. Although these three verses do not contain the argumentative thrust of the previous verses, they play a significant part in completing the section. **Bound** (ὀφείλομεν) or *obligated* is the same term as in 1:3. **Beloved** speaks of *having been and continuing to be loved by God* (ἠγα-πημένοι). The remainder of this verse is debated regarding its content. The manuscripts differ: (1) God chose you as *first fruits* unto salvation...., (2) God chose you *from the beginning*, or (3) God chose you *to himself from the beginning*. The first option "is slightly stronger" in evidence (Bruce). It is also noteworthy that Paul calls initial converts in any place, first fruits (Ro 16:5; 1 Cor 16:15, **the house of Stephanas, that it is the first fruits of Achaia**). The second option strongly suggests "pretemporal election": an unsupported and refuted theological position. The third option has only one manuscript as evidence (88, 12th century). The manuscript evidence and theological evidence leans toward option 1. This **salvation** (σωτηρίαν) is accomplished *by means of making holy* (**sanctification**) *by* the Spirit and *by means of faith in* the truth (Titus 3:5; Eph 1:13, **the word of truth, the gospel of your salvation....**).
[14] **Whereunto** or *concerning which* (referring to salvation) he *summoned* you *through* our gospel to (for the purpose of you becoming) *become a glorious possession of our Lord Jesus Christ* (Eph 1:14). There exist many gospels, yet only one true and efficacious (Ga 1:6-7a). Note that it is by means of the gospel that one becomes a possession of God, not by means of predetermined selection. *Blessed be God and the Father of our Lord Jesus Christ, the one who blessed us with every spiritual blessing in the heavens in Christ, just as He chose us to be with him... in love setting a boundary about us unto sonship, by the agency of Jesus Christ* (Eph 1:4-5).
[15][π] The conclusion of the topic section naturally contains directives concerning the issue. The discussion now turns to duty. *Then* **therefore** (ἄρα οὖν), **brethren**, *take your stand and grasp, grab onto* (κρατεῖτε) **the traditions which you** *were* **taught, whether by word,** *whether by* **our epistle**. This comprises Paul's visit and the first letter. To **stand** (στήκετε) is a common motif in Paul's letters. **To freedom Christ freed us, stand therefore, and be not made subject again to the yoke of bondage** (Ga 5:1)(Phil 1:27; Ro 14:4; 1 Cor 16:13).

GREEK TEXT

[16][π] Αὐτὸς δὲ ὁ κύριος ἡμῶν Ἰησοῦς Χριστὸς καὶ [ὁ] θεὸς ὁ πατὴρ ἡμῶν, ὁ ἀγαπήσας ἡμᾶς καὶ δοὺς παράκλησιν αἰωνίαν καὶ ἐλπίδα ἀγαθὴν ἐν χάριτι, [17] παρακαλέσαι ὑμῶν τὰς καρδίας καὶ στηρίξαι ἐν παντὶ ἔργῳ καὶ λόγῳ ἀγαθῷ.

REFERENCES

[17]
(Ro 1:11) For I long to see you, that I may impart unto you some spiritual gift, to the end you may be established;
(Rev 3:2) Be watchful, and strengthen the things which remain, that are ready to die: for I have not found your works perfect before God.

2 THESSALONIANS 2:16-17

*Verses sixteen and seventeen contain
the first of three
prayer-wishes in the letter.
They are called wishes since they use the optative
(Latin, optari– to wish) mood in Greek.
In this letter, they are used in indirect prayers
where the author tells the reader what he prays for.
This prayer wish is directly connected to the preceding
context and completes the discussion.*

[2:16-17]
[16][π] Now our Lord Jesus Christ himself, and God, even our Father, who has loved us, and has given us everlasting consolation and good hope through grace, [17] Comfort your hearts, and establish you in every good word and work.

[16][π] The two personages, **our Lord Jesus and our Father**, are characterized by their actions: loving and giving. The pronoun *who* (**which**) keys the digression. Note the content of the digression as it relates to the topic. They **have loved** the Thessalonians. They **have given** the Thessalonians an **everlasting consolation** (παράκλησιν) or *everlasting encouragement* (NAB): *eternal comfort* (NASB). Further, a **good hope** or *certain satisfaction* was theirs *by* grace. Contrast this message with their situation- **We beseech you brethren… that you be not shaken… troubled**…. (2:1-2). This 'triangular' prayer (Paul to God for them) brings to light what God has done and will do, contrasting how the Thessalonians were troubled and confused regarding their present situation. This letter served as substantial medicine for the ailments that false teachings had caused.

[17] **Comfort** (παρακαλέσαι) has its subjects from verse sixteen. *The Lord Jesus and God our Father, may he comfort your hearts and may he strengthen* (**establish**, Ro 1:11; Rev 3:2) *you in every work and good word.*

*The next section is the last
major section of the body.
It is called the Parenesis, referring to exhortations,
usually in the form of commands.*

Distribution of Commands		
OPENING	Prescript / Exordium	0
BODY	Topic	2
	Parenesis (Exhortatio)	5
CLOSING	Post Script	0

GREEK TEXT

[1][π] Τὸ λοιπὸν προσεύχεσθε, ἀδελφοί, περὶ ἡμῶν, ἵνα ὁ λόγος τοῦ κυρίου τρέχῃ καὶ δοξάζηται καθὼς καὶ πρὸς ὑμᾶς, [2] καὶ ἵνα ῥυσθῶμεν ἀπὸ τῶν ἀτόπων καὶ πονηρῶν ἀνθρώπων· οὐ γὰρ πάντων ἡ πίστις. [3] πιστὸς δέ ἐστιν ὁ κύριος, ὃς στηρίξει ὑμᾶς καὶ φυλάξει ἀπὸ τοῦ πονηροῦ.

REFERENCES

[1]
(Phil 3:1) Finally, my brethren, rejoice in the Lord. To write the same things to you, to me indeed is not grievous, but for you it is safe.
[2]
(2 Cor 4:17) For our light affliction, which is but for a moment, works for us a far more exceeding and eternal weight of glory;
(2 Cor 11:22 -33) Are they Hebrews? so am I. Are they Israelites? so am I. Are they the seed of Abraham? so am I. [23] Are they ministers of Christ? (I speak as a fool) I am more; in labors more abundant, in stripes above measure, in prisons more frequent, in deaths oft. [24] Of the Jews five times received I forty stripes save one. [25] Thrice was I beaten with rods, once was I stoned, thrice I suffered shipwreck, a night and a day I have been in the deep; [26] In journeyings often, in perils of waters, in perils of robbers, in perils by mine own countrymen, in perils by the heathen, in perils in the city, in perils in the wilderness, in perils in the sea, in perils among false brethren; [27] In weariness and painfulness, in watchings often, in hunger and thirst, in fastings often, in cold and nakedness. [28] Beside those things that are without, that which cometh upon me daily, the care of all the churches. [29] Who is weak, and I am not weak? who is offended, and I burn not? [30] If I must needs glory, I will glory of the things which concern mine infirmities. [31] The God and Father of our Lord Jesus Christ, who is blessed for evermore, knows that I lie not. [32] In Damascus the governor under Aretas the king kept the city of the damascenes with a garrison, desirous to apprehend me: [33] And through a window in a basket was I let down by the wall, and escaped his hands.

2 THESSALONIANS 3:1-3

Verses one through four begin the exhortations.
It is common for the parenetic section to
follow the topic section. This section is fairly easy
to locate because of the frequency of commands.
Paul begins generally and personally.

[3:1-3]
[1][π] Finally, brethren, pray for us, that the word of the Lord may have free course, and be glorified, even as it is with you:
[2] And that we may be delivered from unreasonable and wicked men: for all men have not faith.
[3] But the Lord is faithful, who shall establish you, and keep you from evil.

[1][π] **Finally** (Τὸ λοιπὸν) indicates an impending conclusion. With the topic having been concluded (chapter 2), Paul now begins to bring the letter to an end (Phil 3:1). Paul commands **prayer** regarding the success of the *message* (ὁ λόγος) of the Lord (**And the Word was made flesh, and dwelt among us,** Jn 1:14), that it might *run* (**free course,** *treko*) *and might be* **glorified** (δοξάζηται), *just as even it was* (*it did,* NAS/NAB) *to* **you.** The Thessalonians themselves were an example of the advances of the gospel.
[2] The second prayer request regards *rescue* (ῥυσθῶμεν) from those **wicked men** who would hinder the work. Here, **wicked** (πονηρῶν) and **unreasonable** depict the same type of individuals bent on persecuting the work. The word **unreasonable** (ἀτόπων) literally means *out of place.* Many translations render it as *perverse.* **Alexander the coppersmith did me much evil: the Lord reward him according to his works** (2 Tim 4:14). Perhaps Paul's pre-conversion life might serve as a suitable example of those to be rescued from. **For you have heard of my conversation in time past in the Jews' religion, how that beyond measure I persecuted the church of God, and wasted it.** (Ga 1:13). An understatement undergirds the need for protective prayer, *for not of all [men] is the faith.* Paul's prayer places eternal issues first— the success of **the word of the Lord.** Issues of **light affliction** are placed second (2 Cor 4:17). Paul catalogs some ministry difficulties in 2 Cor 11:24-26, **Of the Jews five times received I forty stripes save one... in perils by mine own country men, in perils by the heathen, in perils in the city, in perils in the wilderness... in perils among false brethren.**
[3] Upon requesting prayer for the difficulties of ministry work, Paul states his confidence that the **Lord is faithful.** His watch-care is to be relied on. With confidence he says the Lord **shall establish** or *strengthen* (στηρίξει) them. He also *shall guard* (φυλάξει) them from *the Evil One* (not evil, note the article, τοῦ πονηροῦ), i.e., the Devil.

GREEK TEXT

[3] πιστὸς δέ ἐστιν ὁ κύριος, ὃς στηρίξει ὑμᾶς καὶ φυλάξει ἀπὸ τοῦ πονηροῦ. [4] πεποίθαμεν δὲ ἐν κυρίῳ ἐφ' ὑμᾶς, ὅτι ἃ παραγγέλλομεν [καὶ] ποιεῖτε καὶ ποιήσετε. [5][π] Ὁ δὲ κύριος κατευθύναι ὑμῶν τὰς καρδίας εἰς τὴν ἀγάπην τοῦ θεοῦ καὶ εἰς τὴν ὑπομονὴν τοῦ Χριστοῦ.

[6][π] Παραγγέλλομεν δὲ ὑμῖν, ἀδελφοί, ἐν ὀνόματι τοῦ κυρίου |omit| [UBS, ἡμῶν] Ἰησοῦ Χριστοῦ, στέλλεσθαι ὑμᾶς ἀπὸ παντὸς ἀδελφοῦ ἀτάκτως περιπατοῦντος καὶ μὴ κατὰ τὴν παράδοσιν ἣν |παρελάβετε| [UBS, παρελάβοσαν] παρ' ἡμῶν.

REFERENCES

[5]
(Heb 12:3) For consider him that endured such contradiction of sinners against himself, lest you be wearied and faint in your minds.
[6]
(1 Cor 7:10) And unto the married I command, yet not I, but the Lord, Let not the wife depart from her husband:
(1 Cor 7:25) Now concerning virgins I have no commandment of the Lord: yet I give my judgment, as one that hath obtained mercy of the Lord to be faithful.
(2 Cor 8:20) Avoiding this, that no man should blame us in this abundance which is administered by us:
(I Cor 5:9 -11) I wrote unto you in an epistle not to company with fornicators: [10] Yet not altogether with the fornicators of this world, or with the covetous, or extortioners, or with idolaters; for then must ye needs go out of the world. [11] But now I have written unto you not to keep company, if any man that is called a brother be a fornicator, or covetous, or an idolater, or a railer, or a drunkard, or an extortioner; with such an one no not to eat.

[3:4-6]
[4] And we have con-
fidence in the Lord
touching you, that you
both do and will do
the things which we
command you.
[5][π] And the Lord
direct your hearts into
the love of God, and
into the patient
waiting for Christ.
[6][π] Now we com-
mand you, brethren, in
the name of our Lord
Jesus Christ, that you
withdraw yourselves
from every brother
that walks disorderly
and not after the
tradition which he
received of us.

[4] *And we have become and continue to be persuaded by the Lord concerning you, that, that which we are charging [you], you are both doing and you shall do.* Such positive avenues of influence, like this vote of confidence, are found throughout Paul's letters. They are the norm.

Verse five contains the second of three prayer-wishes in this epistle. This avenue of influence– the use of wishes, must fill some particular need in Paul's relationship with the Thessalonians. In these two letters, we find five prayer-wishes. Consider that of the 28,121 verbs in the N.T., only 39 are classed as "wish" optatives (0.0014%)(GTJ, Vol. 9, No. 1.).

[5][π] **And** is better *now* (δὲ). *Now, may the Lord direct your hearts unto* (into) *the love of God and unto* (into) *the endurance of Christ.* The phrase **love of God** denotes living under the favor of God's love. The second phrase, **the patience waiting for Christ**, speaks of the endurance which Christ exhibited. Bruce notes, "The patience or steadfastness which Christ displayed should be reproduced in his followers; indeed, he may be said to impart it to them. As he 'endured from sinners such hostility against himself' (Heb 12:3) so should they; indeed, they were already learning to do so (1:4)." The words **waiting for** are not found in the Greek text. They are omitted in the NAS, NASB, NAB, NIV, Rheims and the NRSV. Apparently, an interpretive element has been added. His wish regards the care of God's love and living under difficult situations with the *endurance* (ὑπο-μονὴν) that Christ exemplified.

Verses six through fifteen are a specific section of exhortations. Paul addresses an actual situation in progress at Thessalonica. The directives are pointed and authoritative.

[6][π] **Now... brethren** (δὲ... ἀδελφοί) shows a distinct beginning. The authority cited for the command- **the name of our Lord Jesus Christ** (1 Cor 7:10, 25). The content of the command- *for* **you to withdraw** (*avoiding,* στέλλεσθαι, 2 Cor 8:20) **yourselves from every brother** (friends? associates?)

GREEK TEXT

[6][π] Παραγγέλλομεν δὲ ὑμῖν, ἀδελφοί, ἐν ὀνόματι τοῦ κυρίου |omit| [UBS, ἡμῶν] Ἰησοῦ Χριστοῦ, στέλλεσθαι ὑμᾶς ἀπὸ παντὸς ἀδελφοῦ ἀτάκτως περιπατοῦντος καὶ μὴ κατὰ τὴν παράδοσιν ἣν |παρελάβετε| [UBS, παρελάβοσαν] παρ' ἡμῶν. [7] αὐτοὶ γὰρ οἴδατε πῶς δεῖ μιμεῖσθαι ἡμᾶς, ὅτι οὐκ ἠτακτήσαμεν ἐν ὑμῖν [8] οὐδὲ δωρεὰν ἄρτον ἐφάγομεν παρά τινος, ἀλλ' ἐν κόπῳ καὶ μόχθῳ νυκτὸς καὶ ἡμέρας ἐργαζόμενοι πρὸς τὸ μὴ ἐπιβαρῆσαί τινα ὑμῶν: [9] οὐχ ὅτι οὐκ ἔχομεν ἐξουσίαν, ἀλλ' ἵνα ἑαυτοὺς τύπον δῶμεν ὑμῖν εἰς τὸ μιμεῖσθαι ἡμᾶς. [10] καὶ γὰρ ὅτε ἦμεν πρὸς ὑμᾶς, τοῦτο παρηγγέλλομεν ὑμῖν, ὅτι εἴ τις οὐ θέλει ἐργάζεσθαι μηδὲ ἐσθιέτω.

REFERENCES

[6]

(I Cor 5:9 -11) I wrote unto you in an epistle not to company with fornicators: [10] Yet not altogether with the fornicators of this world, or with the covetous, or extortioners, or with idolaters; for then must your needs go out of the world. [11] But now I have written unto you not to keep company, if any man that is called a brother be a fornicator, or covetous, or an idolater, or a railer, or a drunkard, or an extortioner; with such an one no not to eat.

[7]

(Jn 3:7) Marvel not that I said unto you, You must be born again.

(1 Pet 5:3) Neither as being lords over God's heritage, but being examples to the flock.

[9]

(1 Cor 9:14) Even so hath the Lord ordained that they which preach the gospel should live of the gospel.

[10]

(Ga 6:5) For every man shall bear his own burden.

(Ac 2:43 -47) And they continued steadfastly in the apostles' doctrine and fellowship, and in breaking of bread, and in prayers. [43] And fear came upon every soul: and many wonders and signs were done by the apostles. [44] And all that believed were together, and had all things common; [45] And sold their possessions and goods, and parted them to all men, as every man had need. [46] And they, continuing daily with one accord in the temple, and breaking bread from house to house, did eat their meat with gladness and singleness of heart, [47] Praising God, and having favor with all the people. And the Lord added to the church daily such as should be saved.

[3:6-10]
[6][π] Now we command you, brethren, in the name of our Lord Jesus Christ, that ye withdraw yourselves from every brother that walks disorderly, and not after the tradition which he received of us.
[7] For yourselves know how you ought to follow us: for we behaved not ourselves disorderly among you;
[8] Neither did we eat any man's bread for nought; but wrought with labor and travail night and day, that we might not be chargeable to any of you:
[9] Not because we have not power, but to make ourselves an example unto you to follow us.
[10] For even when we were with you, this we commanded you, that if any would not work, neither should he eat.

who continually **walks disorderly**. The term **walk** (περιπατοῦντος) denotes walk of life or lifestyle. It is in the present tense, telling of continuous life patterns. The adverb **disorderly** (*unsubject*, ἀτάκτως) is broad, denoting any lifestyle in disharmony with clear biblical teaching (1 Cor 5:9ff). Although many see the word **disorderly** as synonymous with laziness (*idle*, NIV), this is not supported by the text or a careful study of the word. Paul has used this term in the first letter; **warn them that are unruly** (5:14). The next clause exposes disorderly as a broad term- **and not** *in accord* **with the tradition which he received of us. Tradition** (παράδοσιν) encompasses doctrine and corresponding behavior, far more than just idleness.

[7] The support (**for**) for the charge- **you yourselves** (intensive form, αὐτοὶ) **know how** *it is mandatory* (δεῖ, Jn 3:7) *for us to be imitated*. A further support (**for**) uses the verb form of **disorderly** (ἠτακτήσαμεν). Paul's team did not set an example for the deviant conduct occurring in the church at Thessalonica (1 Pet 5:3).

[8] *Neither were we eating free bread from any one, but on the contrary, in labor and toil working night and day so that to not burden any of you.* **Any man's bread** seems to be idiomatic for food. It appears that Paul and his team preferred to earn their living from manual labor. This set an example and kept them from any hint of being a ministry for profit initiative.

[9] *It is not that we are having not the authority,* i.e., we both then and now have had the authority to not do manual labor for food. This rightful privilege (1 Cor 9:14) was spurned so that they could render a visible and incontrovertible **example** (Gk., *typos*) to be *duplicated* or *mimicked* (μιμεῖσθαι) in the new converts. Example speaks louder than words.

[10] The argument intensifies and become more personal- **for even when we were with you, this we commanded**.... Paul had given previous information regarding the possibility of such a situation. **If any** *is not willing* (οὐ θέλει) *to work* identifies the problem. Some were refusing to do their part (Ga 6:5). The prescribed response- *don't even allow him to eat*. This is a command, not an option. Compassion on the irresponsible is inappropriate. This severity builds character. What does this command indicate regarding their living situation? It seems to suggest at least a cooperative

GREEK TEXT

[11] ἀκούομεν γὰρ τινας περιπατοῦντας ἐν ὑμῖν ἀτάκτως, μηδὲν ἐργαζομένους ἀλλὰ περιεργαζομένους·

[12][π] τοῖς δὲ τοιούτοις παραγγέλλομεν καὶ παρακαλοῦμεν ἐν κυρίῳ Ἰησοῦ Χριστῷ ἵνα μετὰ ἡσυχίας ἐργαζόμενοι τὸν ἑαυτῶν ἄρτον ἐσθίωσιν. [13] Ὑμεῖς δέ, ἀδελφοί, μὴ ἐγκακήσητε καλοποιοῦντες.

REFERENCES

[12]

(Ro 16:18) For they that are such serve not our Lord Jesus Christ, but their own belly; and by good words and fair speeches deceive the hearts of the simple.

(Ga 5:21) Envyings, murders, drunkenness, revellings, and such like: of the which I tell you before, as I have also told you in time past, that they which do such things shall not inherit the kingdom of God.

[13]

(2 Cor 4:16 -17) For which cause we faint not; but though our outward man perish, yet the inward man is renewed day by day. [17] For our light affliction, which is but for a moment, works for us a far more exceeding and eternal weight of glory;

arrangement, if not a communal situation; **And all that believed were together, and had all things common; And sold their possessions and goods, and parted them to all men, as every man had need** (Ac 2:42-47).

[3:11-13]
[11] For we hear that there are some which walk among you disorderly, working not at all, but are busybodies.
[12][π] Now them that are such we command and exhort by our Lord Jesus Christ, that with quietness they work, and eat their own bread.
[13] But you, brethren, be not weary in well doing.

[11] Paul not only had heard but *was hearing* (ἀκούομεν) the report of problems. The word **disorderly** again appears. It is expanded positively and negatively. **Some** (τινας), not all, are *not even working* (ἐργαζομένους), *but on the contrary, are working in circles* or *circumventing work* (**busybodies**, περιεργαζομένους). Note the word play. The word busybodies seems to indicate those who are busy working, doing nothing of substance.

[Excursus: It is an old view that the "disorderly" who were identified as idlers, are those who sat about waiting for the Lord to come. It is proposed that since Paul said so much regarding the rapture in 1 Thessalonians and that he expected it in his lifetime (did he?), this motivated some to sit and wait. There seems to be no internal evidence in these letters to support this assertion.]

Jesus must be Lord of our relationships.

[12][π] Having discussed the situation (vv 6-11), Paul now directs his writing to those living disorderly. **Now** (δὲ) points to a new division. The word translated **them that are such** (τοιούτοις) seems to find its way into passages regarding problem people. It is used to broaden the application (Ro 16:18; Ga 5:21). They are **commanded** (παραγγέλλομεν) **and exhorted** (παρακαλοῦμεν) by the authority of **our Lord Jesus Christ**. Perhaps **with quietness** (μετὰ ἡσυχίας) means without distracting others or attracting attention. Neil sums it up, "...stop idling, stop sponging". They should be working so that they might eat **their own bread**, i.e., provide for themselves and do their part (v 8). A holy walk of life is a life characterized by rigorous efforts and responsibility.

[13] Paul turns to those who are busy in the work of ministry. Emphatically, **But, YOU brethren,** *do not grow* **weary** (μὴ ἐγκακήσητε, 2 Cor 4:16-17) *in doing good.* "Exhortations to perseverance are common in Paul's writings" (Bruce). Here, the contrast (**but**) is instructive, directing a course of action not adversely affected by the problems about them. The doing of good must continue without distraction.

GREEK TEXT

[14][π] εἰ δέ τις οὐχ ὑπακούει τῷ λόγῳ ἡμῶν διὰ τῆς ἐπιστολῆς, τοῦτον σημειοῦσθε, μὴ συναναμίγνυσθαι αὐτῷ, ἵνα ἐντραπῇ· [15] καὶ μὴ ὡς ἐχθρὸν ἡγεῖσθε, ἀλλὰ νουθετεῖτε ὡς ἀδελφόν.

[16][π] Αὐτὸς δὲ ὁ κύριος τῆς εἰρήνης δῴη ὑμῖν τὴν εἰρήνην διὰ παντὸς ἐν παντὶ τρόπῳ. ὁ κύριος μετὰ πάντων ὑμῶν.

[17][π] Ὁ ἀσπασμὸς τῇ ἐμῇ χειρὶ Παύλου, ὅ ἐστιν σημεῖον ἐν πάσῃ ἐπιστολῇ· οὕτως γράφω.

[18][π] ἡ χάρις τοῦ κυρίου ἡμῶν Ἰησοῦ Χριστοῦ μετὰ πάντων ὑμῶν.

REFERENCES

[14]

(1 Cor 5:9) I wrote unto you in an epistle not to company with fornicators:

(1 Cor 5:11) But now I have written unto you not to keep company, if any man that is called a brother be a fornicator, or covetous, or an idolator, or a railer, or a drunkard, or an extortioner; with such an one no not to eat.

(Ro 16:17) Now I beseech you, brethren, mark them which cause divisions and offences contrary to the doctrine which you have learned; and avoid them.

[18]

(1 Thes 5:28) The grace of our Lord Jesus Christ be with you. Amen.

[3:14-18]
[14][π] And if any man obey not our word by this epistle, note that man, and have no company with him, that he may be ashamed.
[15] Yet count him not as an enemy, but admonish him as a brother.
[16][π] Now the Lord of peace himself give you peace always by all means. The Lord be with you all.
[17][π] The salutation of Paul with mine own hand, which is the token in every epistle: so I write.
[18][π] The grace of our Lord Jesus Christ be with you all. Amen.

[14][π] What if some do not heed the directives of verse twelve, or choose another path of disorder? **And** or *now* (δέ), **if any *does* not obey our word by this epistle** is a very real situation. What must be done? **Note** (σημειοῦσθε), as in *take note of... so that to not have* **company with him**. This word literally means to not *be mixed up with* (συναναμίγνυσθαι) the disobedient brother (1 Cor 5:9, 11; Ro 16:17). The purpose of these actions- *in order* **that he** *might be put to shame* (ἐντραπῆ). What good could this do? Shame can work repentance. The community of believers must not tolerate open disobedience. What is tolerated is embraced.

[15] This verse is not separate from verse fourteen. Paul prohibits, as part of his instructions, **him**, the guilty party, to be *considered* (**count**, ἡγεῖσθε) **as an enemy** (ἐχθρὸν). *On the contrary* (ἀλλὰ, **but**), **admonish** or *warn* (νουθετεῖτε) **him as a brother** (1 Thes. 5:14b). Repentance and restoration of a brother in error is the goal of this directive. He is still family.

Verse sixteen is the fifth and final prayer-wish in the Thessalonian epistles. The vertical and horizontal aspects of this form seem to make this prayer very personal.

[16][π] The final prayer-wish closes out the issue beginning in verse six. The content of all three prayer-wishes relates to what is discussed previously. The fist part of this verse has been summed up as **peace** (*unity?*) " *at all times and in every way*" (1 Thes 5:13, 23). **The Lord be with you all** speaks of the sustaining presence and fellowship of the Lord in their lives.

Verses seventeen and eighteen form the closing of the letter in a postscript. It contains a greeting and a grace wish.

[17][π] The **salutation** or *greeting* (ἀσπασμὸς) **of Paul is** *a sign* (**token**, σημεῖον) of authenticity. This verse tells us that every Pauline epistle had, at least the final greeting(s) in the author's **hand**. Some suggest this would be in the form of an autograph.

[18][π] The final line is nearly identical with 1 Thes 5:28. It requests the *favor* **of the grace of our Lord Jesus Christ**.

APPENDICES:

ALPHA
(PHILEMON SKETCHED IN GREEK:
DIVIDED INTO SENTENCES AND CLAUSES)

BETA
(SELF STUDY CHART
TO BE USED WITH 1 CORINTHIANS)

GAMMA
(BIBLIOGRAPHY)

APPENDIX ALPHA

KEY: The letter Pi [π] is used to show divisions,
sections, and divisions within sections.
Main clauses are in **BOLD**.
Subordinate/Coordinate elements are in ***BOLD ITALIC***.

[1][π]

ΠΑΥΛΟΣ δέσμιος Χριστοῦ Ἰησοῦ καὶ Τιμόθεος ὁ ἀδελφὸς **Φιλήμονι τῷ**
ἀγαπητῷ καὶ συνεργῷ ἡμῶν καὶ Ἀπφίᾳ τῇ ἀδελφῇ καὶ Ἀρχίππῳ τῷ
συστρατιώτῃ ἡμῶν καὶ τῇ κατ' οἶκόν σου ἐκκλησίᾳ·

[3][π]

χάρις ὑμῖν καὶ εἰρήνη ἀπὸ θεοῦ πατρὸς ἡμῶν καὶ κυρίου Ἰησοῦ Χριστοῦ.

[4][π]

Εὐχαριστῶ τῷ θεῷ μου πάντοτε
    μνείαν σου ***ποιούμενος*** ἐπὶ τῶν προσευχῶν μου,
    ἀκούων σου τὴν ἀγάπην καὶ τὴν πίστιν
      ἣν ἔχεις |εἰς| [UBS, πρὸς] τὸν κύριον Ἰησοῦν καὶ εἰς πάντας τοὺς ἁγίους,
      ὅπως ἡ κοινωνία τῆς πίστεώς σου ἐνεργὴς γένηται ἐν ἐπιγνώσει παντὸς
                          ἀγαθοῦ τοῦ ἐν ἡμῖν εἰς Χριστόν:
    χαρὰν ***γὰρ*** πολλὴν ἔσχον καὶ παράκλησιν ἐπὶ τῇ ἀγάπῃ σου,
    ὅτι τὰ σπλάγχνα τῶν ἁγίων ἀναπέπαυται διὰ σοῦ, ἀδελφέ.

[9][π]

    Διό, πολλὴν ἐν Χριστῷ παρρησίαν ***ἔχων*** ἐπιτάσσειν σοι τὸ ἀνῆκον,
διὰ τὴν ἀγάπην μᾶλλον παρακαλῶ, τοιοῦτος ὢν ὡς
            Παῦλος πρεσβύτης, νυνὶ δὲ καὶ δέσμιος Χριστοῦ Ἰησοῦ

[10] **παρακαλῶ σε περὶ τοῦ ἐμοῦ τέκνου,**
    ὃν ἐγέννησα ἐν τοῖς δεσμοῖς Ὀνήσιμον, τόν ποτέ σοι ἄχρηστον
    νυνὶ δὲ [καὶ] σοὶ καὶ ἐμοὶ εὔχρηστον,
    ὃν ἀνέπεμψά σοι, αὐτόν,
      τοῦτ' ἔστιν τὰ ἐμὰ σπλάγχνα:
    ὃν ἐγὼ ἐβουλόμην πρὸς ἐμαυτὸν κατέχειν,
      ἵνα ὑπὲρ σοῦ μοι διακονῇ ἐν τοῖς δεσμοῖς τοῦ εὐαγγελίου,
    χωρὶς ***δὲ*** τῆς σῆς γνώμης οὐδὲν ἠθέλησα ποιῆσαι,
      ἵνα μὴ ὡς κατὰ ἀνάγκην τὸ ἀγαθόν σου ᾖ
        ἀλλὰ [τὸ ἀγαθόν σου ᾖ] κατὰ ἑκούσιον.

[15] τάχα *γὰρ* διὰ τοῦτο ἐχωρίσθη πρὸς ὥραν
    ἵνα αἰώνιον αὐτὸν ἀπέχῃς, οὐκέτι ὡς δοῦλον
    ἀλλ' [αὐτὸν ἀπέχῃς] ὑπὲρ δοῦλον, ἀδελφὸν ἀγαπητόν,
                                     μάλιστα ἐμοί,
    πόσῳ *δὲ* μᾶλλον σοὶ καὶ ἐν σαρκὶ καὶ ἐν κυρίῳ.

[17][π]
    Εἰ οὖν με ἔχεις κοινωνόν,
προσλαβοῦ αὐτὸν ὡς ἐμέ.

    εἰ δέ τι ἠδίκησέν σε
    ἢ ὀφείλει,
τοῦτο ἐμοὶ ἐλλόγα:

[19][π]
ἐγὼ Παῦλος ἔγραψα τῇ ἐμῇ χειρί,

ἐγὼ ἀποτίσω·
    ἵνα μὴ λέγω σοι ὅτι καὶ σεαυτόν μοι προσοφείλεις.

[20][π]
ναί, ἀδελφέ, ἐγώ σου ὀναίμην ἐν κυρίῳ·

ἀνάπαυσόν μου τὰ σπλάγχνα ἐν Χριστῷ.

    Πεποιθὼς τῇ ὑπακοῇ σου
ἔγραψά σοι,
    εἰδὼς ὅτι καὶ ὑπὲρ ἃ λέγω ποιήσεις.

[22][π]
ἅμα *δὲ* καὶ ἑτοίμαζέ μοι ξενίαν,
ἐλπίζω *γὰρ* ὅτι διὰ τῶν προσευχῶν ὑμῶν χαρισθήσομαι ὑμῖν.

[23][π]
Ἀσπάζεταί σε Ἐπαφρᾶς ὁ συναιχμάλωτός μου ἐν Χριστῷ Ἰησοῦ,
Μᾶρκος, Ἀρίσταρχος, Δημᾶς, Λουκᾶς, οἱ συνεργοί μου.

[25][π]
Ἡ χάρις τοῦ κυρίου Ἰησοῦ Χριστοῦ μετὰ τοῦ πνεύματος ὑμῶν.

O P E N I N G	**PRESCRIPT** REFERENCES: (1:1- LIST ELEMENTS: **EXORDIUM** REFERENCES: LIST ELEMENTS:
B O D Y	# TOPIC WHAT VERSE CONTAINS THE DISCLOSURE FORMULA? WHAT IS THE STATED ISSUE IN CORINTH? NOTE THE DIVISIONS WITHIN THE BODY: WHAT IS PAUL'S SOLUTION TO THE ISSUE? **PARENESIS** REFERENCES: LIST DIRECTIVES:
C L O S I N G	REFERENCES: LIST ELEMENTS:

APPENDIX GAMMA

Barclay   William Barclay. *The letters to Timothy, Titus, and Philemon.* (rev. ed.). Philadelphia: Westminster Press, 1960.
William Barclay. *The Letters to the Philippians, Colossians, and Thessalonians* (rev. ed.). Philadelphia: Westminster Press, 1960.

Bicknell   E. J. Bicknell. *The First and Second Epistles to the Thessalonians.* London: Imprint, 1932.

BKC   John Walvoord and Roy Zuch. *The Bible Knowledge Commentary* (N.T.). Wheaton: SP Publications, Inc., 1983.

Bruce   F.F. Bruce. *1 & 2 Thessalonians.* Waco, Texas: Word Books, 1982.

C&H   W.J. Conbeare & J.S. Howson. *The life and Epistles of St. Paul.* Grand Rapids: Eerdmans, 1983.

Eadie   John Eadie. *Commentary on the Greek Text of the Epistles of Paul to the Thessalonians.* Minneapolis: James Pub., 1976.

EBC   Frank E. Gaebelein (Gen. ed.). *The Expositors Bible Commentary.* Grand Rapids: Zondervan, 1976.

Findlay   G. G. Findlay. *The Epistles of Paul the Apostle to the Thessalonians.* Cambridge: University Press, 1904.

Frame   James E. Frame. *A Critical and Exegetical Commentary on the Epistles of St. Paul to the Thessalonians.* New York: Charles Scribner's, 1912.

GTJ   Grace Theological Journal. Editor John C. Whitcomb.

Heibert   D. Edmond Hiebert. *The Thessalonian Epistles.* Chicago: Moody Press, 1971.

Hendriksen   William Hendriksen. *Exposition of I and II Thessalonians.* Grand Rapids: Baker Book House, 1955.

IBC   F.F. Bruce (gen. ed). *The International Bible Commentary.* Grand Rapids: Zondervan, 1986.

Louw   J.P. Louw. *Semantics of New Testament Greek.* Atlanta: Scholars Press, 1982.

Louw/Nida   Johannes Louw and Eugene Nida. *Greek English Lexicon of the N.T.* (2 Vols.). New York: UBS, 1989.

Lightfoot   J. B. Lightfoot. *Colossians and Philemon.* Alister McGrath, J. I. Packer (eds.). Crossway Classic Commentary Series, 1997.

Lohse   Eduard Lohse. *Colossians and Philemon: a Commentary on the Epistle.* Philadelphia: Fortress Press, 1975.

Marshall   I. Howard Marshall. *1 and 2 Thessalonians.* Grand Rapids: Eerdmans, 1983.Bruce

Metzger   Manning Metzger. *The Text of the New Testament* (2nd ed.). New York: Oxford University Press, 1968.

Morris   Leon Morris. *The Epistles of Paul to the Thessalonians.* Grand Rapids: Eerdmans, 1984.

Neil   William Neil. *The Epistle of Paul to the Thessalonians.* New York: Harper, 1950.

NIVBC   Kenneth L. Barker & John R. Kohlenberger III (eds.). *The NIV Bible Commentary*. Vol 2. Grand Rapids, Zondervan, 1994.

Pentecost   J. Dwight Pentecost. *Things to Come*. Grand Rapids: Zondervan, 1964.

Richards   Lawrence O. Richards. *New Testament Life and Times*. Colorado Springs, CO: Cook Communications Ministries, 2002.

Robertson   A.T. Robertson. *Word Pictures in the N.T.* Grand Rapids: Baker, 1931.

A.T. Robertson. *The Minister and His Greek New Testament.* Grand Rapids: Baker, 1978.

Schreiner   Thomas R. Schreiner. *Interpreting the Pauline Epistles.* Grand Rapids: Baker, 1990.

Wanamaker   Charles A. Wanamaker. *The Epistles to the Thessalonians.* Grand Rapids: W.B. Eerdmans, 1990.

WWB   Paul D. Gardner (ed.). *The Complete Who's Who in the Bible.* Grand Rapids: Zondervan, 1995.

Zerwick   Max Zerwick and Mary Grosvenor. *Grammatical Analysis of the Greek New Testament.* Rome: Biblical Institute Press, 1981.

TRANSLATIONS & TEXTS

NAB   *The New American Bible*. Confraternity of Christian Doctrine, Washington, D.C, 1970.

NASB   *The New American Standard Bible*. The Lockman Foundation, 1963.

NIV   *The New International Version*. International Bible Society, 1973.

UBS   *The Greek New Testament* (3rd edition). London: United Bible Societies, 1975.

W/H   Brooke Foss Westcott & Fenton John Anthony Hort. *The New Testament in the Original Greek*. (author's copy). London: Macmillan and Co., 1900.